What the Critics Have Said About Eric Bogosian and DRINKING IN AMERICA

"Those of you who thought you resided in the United States of America are in for a shock: you're actually living—I think almost everyone in the modern world is—in the tiny principality of Bogosian. . . . Like Walt Whitman, he hears America singing, and he contains multitudes enough to sing the song of America through himself. . . ." —MICHAEL FEINGOLD, *The Village Voice*

"Caustic satire at its most potent . . . *Drinking in America* is a gripping, often scalding portrait of the American nightmare."
—*The New York Daily News*

"The most biting black humorist of the decade. . . . It is surprising to see a performer use such a serious subject to make an audience roar laughing." —*Women's Wear Daily*

"Sardonic and uncompromising social commentary. It sinks its teeth deep into America and gives us something to chew on."
—JOHN SIMON, *New York Magazine*

"Cheers for *Drinking!* Insightful and deadly funny."
—*The New York Post*

"*Drinking in America* is a wild, nightmarish ride . . . an unforgettable journey made all the more disturbing because of the laughter the audience encounters along the way." —*Associated Press*

"Gifted, inventive, observant, dynamic! Every word, every gesture, every shiver of Bogosian's world rings true. His American panorama is documentary art, an inspired invention."
—*Gannett Newspapers*

"The writing is not merely jokey . . . at times it can lift off into extravagantly surreal flights."

—Frank Rich, *The New York Times*

"Cold, hard truth . . . is what Bogosian has to offer. He's a major talent with great artistic promise." —*Variety*

"A vivid, harrowing social document, a journey through the American heartland . . . it is the theatrical equivalent of Hunter Thompson's 'Fear and Loathing' writings. . . ."

—*Hollywood Reporter*

"Continuous laughter is the response the audience makes to Bogosian's portrayal of rogues, dolts, hacks, and down-and-outers."

—Brendan Gill, *The New Yorker*

DRINKING IN AMERICA

ERIC BOGOSIAN

DRINKING IN AMERICA

Vintage Books A Division of Random House New York

A Vintage Original,
First Edition, June 1987

Portions of this text originally appeared in *Harper's* and *New York Talk*.

Library of Congress Cataloging in Publication Data
Bogosian, Eric.
Drinking in America.
1. Monologues. I. Title.
PN4305.M6B66 1987 812'.54 86-46189
ISBN 0-394-75067-5

Design by Jo Bonney
Photographs by Paula Court

Manufactured in the United States of America
10 9 8 7 6 5 4 3 2 1

For Jo Anne

Acknowledgments

Without the encouragement and support of the following people, the monologues would not have been born and lived the full life they have led. Thank you.

Frederick Zollo, Wynn Handman, Joseph Papp, Frank and Woji Gero, and my parents, Henry and Edwina Bogosian.

Michael Morris, Tim Carr, Paula Court, Rebecca Green, Phil Rinaldi, Barbara Ligeti, Mark Russell, George Lane, Jonathan Trumper and David Rosenthal.

Jackie Apple, Josh Baer, Sally Banes, Rosetta Brooks, Steven Cohen, Michael Feingold, Roselee Goldberg, Debra Hauer, Jeanne Hedstrom, Lynn Holst, A. Leroy, Robert Longo, Mary MacArthur, Julia Miles, Nick Paleologos, Frank Rich, Robert Riley, V. Tatransky, Van Lagestein, Martha Wilson and Michael Zwack.

I would also like to thank the National Endowment for the Arts, the New York State Council on the Arts and the Beard's Fund for financial assistance during a period when it was most needed.

Special thanks to Jo Anne.

Contents

DRINKING IN AMERICA

INTRODUCTION

I came to New York City to make coffee.

I wanted to be an actor, so, in the fall of 1975, I became a "gofer" at the Chelsea Westside Theater. I made coffee and I watched a semi-avant-garde play get cast, rehearsed, promoted, open, get reviewed (trashed) and close. I saw the director get shit-faced and morose the night the reviews came in. An empty feeling took over as the actors returned to their daytime soap operas and unemployment lines. Show biz. A real learning experience.

"The Ricky Paul Show" with Joe Hannan and George Bishop, August 1980

I lived in the theater, actually an old church on Forty-third Street and Ninth Avenue. I had a foam mat on the floor in the garret, where at night I could peek out the circular window in the roof and watch the straight hookers fight with the transvestite hookers ("Hey baby, three holes is better than two!"). The neighborhood was nothing like the Yuppie paradise it is today, and for laughs I would hang out at an all-night Greek souvlaki shop in Times Square and see hoodlums steal éclairs. Or I'd take a quick spin around the block to check out the goings-on with the local pushers, bag ladies and soapbox preachers. The cultural life was rich: Lincoln Center, Broadway, porno shops, "snuff" movie houses and the Port Authority bus station.

I had come from Woburn, Massachusetts, a fine New England town noted for its rambunctious biker gangs, its indicted and convicted mayors and the worst toxic-waste dumping grounds in the United States. But it's also an old colonial city with a bronze minuteman on the town green guarding the white-shingled Methodist church and a great ivy-covered library with a statue of Count Rumford on its front lawn. There is also no small amount of theatrical tradition. In fact, most of my stage acting has occurred in Woburn, either as a student at Woburn High (under the guidance of drama teacher Dot McCausland, who had the loyalty of her students because she favored plays ending in murder or bloodshed) or, after I graduated, as a member of the now-defunct Woburn Drama Guild.

But now, in New York, I was invisible, invulnerable, a pair of eyes floating through a world of sordid activity created only for my vicarious amusement. Numb with boredom, I would walk out of a half-baked theatrical production of

Hedda Gabler and find all the drama I could stomach on the street. As a suburban boy, born and bred, something deep in my middle-class soul responded to New York City as nothing more than a very imaginative and entertaining movie.

I had to decide what to do with my life. I liked being an actor but knew I wouldn't be able to feed myself. Also, I was having doubts about legitimate theater; what saved me, I guess, was discovering other things going on, especially in SoHo: performance art, video art and so-called experimental theater. I learned about "artists," people who didn't wait for a director, casting agent, acting coach or cabaret owner to get to work. They just did it, and I wanted to, too.

I went to work at The Kitchen as the low man on the totem pole (a step up from gofer) and entered the world of "downtown." I liked it. By the time I arrived, The Kitchen, a large loft on Broome Street, had become a mecca for the international world of performance art, new music and video art; there I witnessed firsthand the most self-indulgent scene since the days of Dada.

The pinnacle of achievement in experimental theater in 1976 was Philip Glass's and Robert Wilson's opera, *Einstein on the Beach*, at the Metropolitan Opera. I was a true believer and sat dutifully in my seat for the full six hours. I found an excitement I couldn't find in traditional theater. *Einstein* was a visual and aural masterpiece, intellectually stimulating, bold, loud, bohemian, young and unfettered by commercial stodginess. After the premiere, we had a party at The Kitchen for the cast; everybody danced with everybody else, got drunk on white wine and gobbled grapes and brie sandwiches paid for with then-plentiful "non-profit" financing from the National Endowment for the Arts and the New York State Council on the Arts. . . . History was being made!

It was an attractive scene, with its emphasis on the conceptual. *Concept, semiotics, minimalism* were the buzz words, Susan Sontag's *Against Interpretation* was the manifesto and Roland Barthes stood above it all as appointed patron saint. It was heady. Art didn't have to be salable, no one really had to understand it and sometimes you didn't even have to make it in the first place. The main prerequisite was that art be imaginative. Works were not concerned with specific "content," rather with "ways of seeing."

In the warm wash of a post-Vietnam, semihippie, semipolitical atmosphere, this all made sense and seemed significant. I found the "Give My Regards to Broadway" stance of theater like *A Chorus Line* and *The Wiz* repellent; what I needed was something that reflected my state of mind, something like Richard Foreman's seminude, manic nightmare landscapes or Joan Jonas's black velvet and Benzedrine solos or Vito Acconci's lyrical, almost silly, masochism. . . .

But there were contradictions. I would hang out in the viewing room of the Whitney Museum and force myself to watch films of abstract flashing color, convinced the Whitney wouldn't show such hogwash unless it had some significance. I would tour the galleries, unaware of the politics behind the display of the powerful and the connected. I would sit patiently at New Music and Experimental Dance concerts (always on a cushion on the floor) until my ass ached, waiting for the good part. Something had to be there. *Artforum* said so.

I had my doubts, but who was counting? . . . Especially since the appeal was as social as it was esthetic. I liked the "life-style" of the art crowd. Theater people didn't seem to be having fun. Being in theater meant getting head shots, going through the pain of auditions, the humiliation of looking for an agent, taking classes from some deadbeat and waiting tables. My philosophy of life (based on the possibility of an imminent fatal truck accident) did not allow for so much industry with such a high risk for failure. And anyway, making it in theater show business meant . . . what? Getting on a soap? Being cast in a play that the New York critics would eat for breakfast? I wanted to have fun *now* and make work that excited me *now*. As Paul "Crocodile Dundee" Hogan says: "Life is not a dress rehearsal. . . ."

So, my misgivings aside, my life "downtown" continued. My art, music and dance friends, too young to be taken seriously by the "avant-garde" art establishment, were crowding into CBGB's, Max's, the Ocean Club, and Hurrah's (later the Mudd, Tier 3, Irving Plaza, Club 57) to see and hear the Dead Boys, Television, Talking Heads, X-Ray Spex, the Ramones (later James Chance and the Contortions, Teenage Jesus and the Jerks, the Pretenders, the B-52's, the Screamers, Rhys Chatham and Glenn Branca). Movies, as opposed to films, were taken very seriously: *Apocalypse Now*, *Raging Bull*, and any new work by Eric Mitchell, James Nares, Beth B and Scott B.

It was, it seemed, a new way to thrive. "My life is my art" may sound pretentious, but it's a great way to pass the time.

Big doses of sex, drugs and rock-and-roll were necessary for a fertile ground in which to plant young art seeds. This burn-the-candle-at-both-ends philosophy had little to do with the reigning SoHo loft/bean sprouts/granola/conceptual art scene. To go round the clock nonstop was the unspoken credo of my generation. You had to work at a job, work on your art, talk about the art, go to all the shows, all the films, all the clubs, dance all night and have some kind of sex life, too.

We were the new kids in town, the ones with the TV- and rock-and-roll-addled brains. David Byrne said "stay hungry" and that wasn't hard. The grants were drying up, the economy sucked, there was no place to live and the notion of a fashionable "avant-garde" was passé for the moment. You got on the guest list at the nightclubs, you dressed in black, you sniped up posters in the middle of the night for your latest production and scammed whatever mood changers you could find. You were tired all the time and your refrigerator contained nothing but a half-empty jar of mustard, an onion and part of a six-pack. And everybody you knew was either in a band or an artist or a dancer. (No actors allowed.) Reality was setting in: if we weren't anything like the old SoHoites with their down parkas, whole wheat bread, futons on the floor and trips to India, why should we like their art?

Something was itching to get out. I was trying to make performance art, since it seemed in its naïve way a primal form of theater. At its best, it had an energy I couldn't find in commercial theater. It had moments. So I made slides and tape loops. I tried to make the most conceptual stuff I could, with, of course, a strong emphasis on imagination.

My friends came, people who owed no allegiance to what was good or bad in theater, people who simply liked it or didn't. I wrote things like this, a piece called "Garden," from 1978:

A man is standing on a metal ramp in the middle of the performance space. He paces as he recites.

This is my place. Welcome to my place.
Lessons to be learned.
First of all, keep everything under control.
Secondly, you can't make any mistakes.
Third: Compromise is unacceptable.
Four: The rules must be followed.
Five: Perfection exists.
Six: You must be careful.
Seven: You must be reluctant.
Eight: All parts fit together perfectly.
Nine: This is knowledge.
Ten: Imperfection cannot be tolerated.
Eleven: All crime will be punished, all criminals destroyed.
Twelve: Hate is a revelation of weakness.
Thirteen: As it appears, so it is.
Fourteen: Laxity breeds disaster.
Fifteen: The task of the teacher is a difficult one.
Sixteen: Any breach of vigilance is a vulnerability.
Seventeen: The world is made of many parts.
Eighteen: Love is the key to redemption and power.
Nineteen: A single goal makes all men brothers.
Twenty: Precision lies between all things.
Twenty-one: Every gesture must be final.
Twenty-two: The law provides transcendence.
Twenty-three: You must take care in the actions.
Twenty-four: There is no middle ground.
Twenty-five: Sacrifice is the greatest glory.
Twenty-six: Strength comes through patience.
Twenty-seven: There exists a final order.

Twenty-eight: Beauty lies in the eye of the beholder.
Twenty-nine: Possession is a myth.
Thirty: Most choices will never be made.
Thirty-one: The unity of the will makes theheart secure.
Thirty-two: The day will come.
Thirty-three: This is where we are. It is the only place.
Thirty-four: You must never be ready.
Thirty-five: To possess is to see clearly.
Thirty-six: Gifts must be given.
Thirty-seven: The sin of imperfection is claimed by destruction.
Thirty-eight: Complete exposure brings complete fulfillment.
Thirty-nine: The roles have been assigned.
Forty: Now is the time for all good men to rejoice.
Forty-one: He who hesitates is forgotten.
Forty-two: Peace comes through suffering.
Forty-three: All errors surface eventually.
Forty-four: Something does not fit—remove it.
Forty-five: Do what you know is right.
Forty-six: Ignorance is chaos.
Forty-seven: Imitation brings understanding.
Forty-eight: Weakness has no purpose.
Forty-nine: The design will reveal itself.
Fifty: Passion has no virtue.
Fifty-one: Every movement must be accounted for.
Fifty-two: Ecstasy is never known.
Fifty-three: There is no alternative.
Fifty-four: To cut away is to reveal.
Fifty-five: All choice is fiction.
Fifty-six: The signs are there for all to see.
Fifty-seven: The knowledge of all men is based in fact.
Fifty-eight: And after knowledge, there is nothing.
Fifty-nine: There is a place for every man.
Sixty: He that endures until the end, he shall be saved.
Sixty-one: Every movement has a purpose.
Sixty-two: The love of many shall wax cold.
Sixty-three: To touch is to destroy.
Sixty-four: All sins will be seen.
Sixty-five: The judgment will renounce the undecided.
Sixty-six: Progress is foremost.
Sixty-seven: The reward is not easily gained.
Sixty-eight: Clarity is a way of life.

> Sixty-nine: An order will be established and it will unite.
> Seventy: The limits are realized when they are broken.
> Seventy-one: All that can be seen can be mea sured.
> Seventy-two: And after all, it comes to this.
> Seventy-three: To forgive is to weaken.
> Seventy-four: Some can be taught, some must be led.
> Seventy-five: Courage is born in destruction.
> Seventy-six: Only the flawless is justified.
> Seventy-seven: Some must be separated.
> Seventy-eight: Inattention is the greatest sin.
> Seventy-nine: The greatest burden is carried by the able.
> Eighty: The rules are clear.

I recited all this from memory before a dumbfounded audience of maybe thirty in a small loft on Franklin Street. The entire performance took place on top of a large metal-and-wood ramp I had constructed. It was not the kind of thing you did at a comedy club like Catch a Rising Star. Nor was this, a monologue I called "The Day Will Come," from 1977:

Heard over the loudspeaker system. A cultured, soft-spoken woman's voice.

> The day will come. The day will come when there will be a reckoning: an adding up and totaling. Those who turned away will be turned upon. The walls will tumble and blood will coat the cobblestones of your lovely little village. There cannot be oppression without oppressors, so heed this message and hear your well-earned fate: You turned away and said it was beyond understanding; you said you were helpless and confused. But you knew, you knew very well, so know this now as you sip your Perrier and smooth your velvet pants.

. . .

I don't care what your story is. You are responsible and there will be no confusion at the trial. It will be short and necks will crack. On the day the sun will rise and you will fall to your knees. The whips will strip your back bare to the bone. Your children will cry for you as they are slaughtered before your eyes. You will kneel in their blood. Your teeth will break against each other, but you will not cry, for there will be no one to hear you. Your nostrils will ache with the smell of bloated death and drying blood. You will be bound and filled with sickness. Infested with disease, your limbs will drop from your body like wet loaves of bread. . . .

You know why . . . you know what you did. . . . Your unending last sight will be of the dogs that will come to feed upon you. You will live and die at the same time and you will know the day.

And if you are not ripped to shreds by the downtrodden who have wasted their lives for your sake, life itself will come to visit and demand payment.

You will get old. You will bow and creep upon the streets for all to mock. You will become sick and hope to die. Day and night will become one and fear will be your only emotion. You will know nothing and the darkness will hold you tight. You will cry, but no tears will come. You will run and fall. You will crawl, but not in enough time.

Your blindness will let you see only each waiting danger, while it bars your escape. Your body will be your enemy and your intestines will wrap around your heart and take your breath away.

The guns will come. The knives and clubs will come. The razors and broken bottles. The chains and ropes. The hangings. The electric wires. The twisted arms. The broken legs. The drowning faces. The bound eyes. The broken teeth. The ripped ears. The rape. The midnight rides. The damp cells. The people you do not know who want to be inside you. The guns will come.

> The gentle will go first. The gentle who would not speak. You. The artists. You will hang high over the streets. You will be buried in piles. You will dig your own hole. You will starve and cry. You will suck your own running sores. You will cower. You will have no thoughts and your punishment will be holier than a pope's funeral.
>
> Whether rising tide overcomes you or whether your very body becomes your torturer, you will not escape. What awaits you worst of all, is the ultimate prison, the one you made yourself; the ultimate solitude. Your own hand laid the bricks, and there is not time now to leave this favorite place. Your prison has walls one hundred feet thick and not a rat to keep you company.
>
> I am not angry with you. You must understand this most of all. But neither would I forgive you. You must do that yourself. I am here merely to tell you that the day will come. . . . It will. . . .
>
> And when it comes it will be so long it will be an eternity's eternity. And you will not escape. You will not escape until you understand that the day will come.

They were rolling in the aisles!

I thought my stuff was great. But I kept wondering why the art world didn't bow to my achievement. The only place I got reviewed was in the *SoHo Weekly News*.

Around this time, I met some visual artists, notably Michael Zwack, Cindy Sherman and Robert Longo, all of whom were working with pictures in a new way that I found exciting and cool. And they thought I was funny! They loved my stuff.

And what was their stuff like? Ironic in the extreme and dependent on letting the pictures—which had a superficial quality that gave them instant impact—tell the story. These artists shared the belief that in our age of mass media we are saturated by imagery, and this familiar imagery, if framed, set off, edited or piled up, can reveal deeper currents flowing within us. In other words, they were slam dancing with pictures.

At the same time, the work was technically well-made, almost obsessive. And (oh, no!) it was *entertaining*. Anything but minimal. It was not expressive; there wasn't anything as broad as "consciousness" or as topical as "politics." It was about the way we of the mass-media generation react and act on what we see.

Jack Goldstein did a performance that was just two guys fencing while music played in the background. Longo made reliefs of men fighting. Cindy loved making photos of stereotyped women. Zwack had a thing for heroic faces. David Salle called his show at The Kitchen *Bearding the Lion in His Den* and that's what it was all about. You wanna look at pictures of violence? sex? pretty girls? romantic landscapes? Fine, we'll give 'em to you. And then we'll twist the whole thing so that you're stuck with WHY you wanna look at 'em.

This was art that turned things inside me. Very smart and overwhelming. I had wanted to make performances about men and women. I wanted to make performances about torture in Chile. But it made no sense to me to lecture my audience. I found the most interesting facet of any subject to be the part I wasn't clear about. Like, "Yeah racism is terrible, so how come at night I cross the street when a black guy is walking toward me?" It was definitely more interesting to explore my personal biases and the questions deep in my gut. No matter how repulsive.

I was challenged by the sparseness of this new work. I had been couching my stuff in very artsy terminology. It was all kind of surreal with the tapes running and the "nonlinear structure." It dawned on me that all of that was rather contrived. Skip it. Get to the point.

So, I created a persona: Ricky Paul. In the guise of a comedian/entertainer, he had nothing positive to say about anybody or anything and reveled in the paranoia and decay of the modern world. And he did this as a "comedian" and as a singer exploding with patter and song at ninety miles an hour. As I wrote Ricky's monologues, I would aim for what would disturb and upset my audiences—and then launch right into their worst fears and prejudices. If I was playing to a college crowd in Massachusetts, I'd talk about how lazy blacks are; for a feminist mother's group in Milwaukee, I'd crack jokes about how "you can't live with 'em and you can't live without 'em"; in Berlin, I goose-stepped across the stage, *sieg heiled*, and asked the audience if the theater I was in was built with American Marshall Plan money.

The desired effect was usually achieved. My performances were greeted by flying bottles, spit and people trying to climb onstage and grab the microphone away; one woman at some artsy benefit actually started beating me when I got offstage. In Boston, a small riot broke out when the bottles proved ineffective. I began to understand the power of the spoken word, especially when uttered in the face of the fragility of people's beliefs. I made them laugh at violence and prejudice, then feel embarrassed for the laughter.

. . .

So there I was, dressed in black all the time, keeping upside-down hours, wearing sunglasses, maintaining an obnoxious public persona, the whole shtik. It was fun . . . but I was impatient with the moronic drunk and coked-up club audiences. And I didn't get the charge I needed from the esoteric "pieces" . . . especially after a show I wrote, directed and performed called "The New World"—involving sixteen scenes and fifteen actors—couldn't snag a review and all the equipment was stolen as we were about to extend the run. I lost all my savings (around two thousand dollars) and was thrown into deep, instant debt.

My love affair with the avant-garde had ended. It was time to get practical. I was out of money, so I had to make work cheap. Solos were the answer. No rehearsal space had to be rented, no actors paid, no costly sets, costumes or lights. And the stuff was portable. Which meant I could tour and instead of losing money, I could make it.

But I didn't want to become Ricky Paul; I wanted the pieces to exist in the theater and, when I went home, I wanted to go home as me. Also, I got the feeling that Ricky's point had been made. It was as if people were waiting for me to do something really outrageous. Like blow my brains out onstage. And the club scene was not satisfying. So you're outrageous and what else do you do?

But I did love Ricky's energy. And I still wanted to create pieces. Looking at the stuff my artist friends produced, I saw the answer: make a gallery of people, each going "all the way" into his world. Individually the characters might be repulsive, unnerving, pathetic or melodramatic, but taken together a large picture could be seen. Like a collage.

But not a dreamy one; rather, a "switching-stations" one. I had enjoyed watching performers like Andy Kaufman and John Wood make lightning changes during a performance, but disliked the presence of the performer "himself." So I just cut out all the in-between stuff. Like you were turning channels: first this guy, then that guy. Fragments. Chunks of personality. There was no need for me to be up there. I borrowed types from television and, from the streets, I grabbed the derelicts, home-boys and punks I had been watching since I had arrived in New York. All I had to add was the energy.

The greatest performers I had seen live were rock stars. Jimi, Mick, Janis—they played to the audience, they used their presence, they went all the way and that's the way I wanted to perform.

Of course, theater isn't rock-and-roll. But I'd seen rock-and-roll energy in a theatrical production enough times to know it could be done: John Wood in *Travesties* (and later John Malkovich and Gary Sinise in *True West*). There were other models: great underground performers like Brother Theodore, Jeff Weiss, James Chance (of the Contortions) and Tomatoe (of the Screamers). And I couldn't ignore Richard Pryor in his first live concert film. Nor De Niro in *Mean Streets*. And let's not forget Jimmy Swaggart!

I had nothing to say to anybody. Only questions. I wanted to rock and I wanted to act. I loved making believe I was somebody else. And I wanted to be an artist. . . .

So I made these pieces, first *Men Inside*, then *Voices of America*, *FunHouse* and most recently *Drinking in Amer-*

ica. They live in my world, are made for my voice and my temperament. They were meant to be performed and never seen again. To work off the audience. I hope you can get the sense of the voices from the printed page. If not, Forty-second and Eighth isn't that far.

DRINKING IN AMERICA

All around me in 1985 I saw a lot of drinking and drugging. Some people fucking their lives up pretty good. And then there were these Yuppies and their "life-style." Time to make a lot of money and have a lot of things. And then there'd been the Los Angeles Olympics. And Grenada.

"Richie" from "Drinking in America," 1986

Power. The American Way. Everybody either getting screwed up, or rich or spiritual. . . . Read a book about John Belushi . . . see a film directed by Sylvester Stallone . . . watch Ronald Reagan give a speech.

And in the middle of this "new age," Eric Bogosian, a "downtown artist" wanting to get a good review in the paper, make a few bucks and possibly go to LA and make a deal. Sounded like good stuff from which to make a solo. . . .

Drinking in America first appeared at the Institute of Contemporary Art in Boston (egged on by Bob Riley). From there it had a short stint at PS 122 in New York City (smiled at by Mark Russell), then went on a tour of Britain (with the help of Michael Morris of the London ICA) and finally came to roost at The American Place Theater, opening in January 1986, where I was directed by Wynn Handman.

Journal

A man stands and reads out loud to the audience in a normal voice. Begin with improvised patter to the effect that this journal was found in an attic with some old college memorabilia.

April 11, 1971
Today I began to understand one of the immutable truths with regard to my own existence. Today I discovered that I am not a being surrounded by walls and barriers, but part of a continuum with all other things, those living and even those inanimate. I feel a new surge of desire for life, for living now, for getting out and becoming part of everything around me. I want to change the world and I know I can do it. I'm like a newborn baby taking his first steps. I was blind before to my inner self, my true desires, my own special powers and the universe itself. So many people live lives of pointless desperation, unable to appreciate that life is life to be lived for today, in every flower, in a cloud . . . in a smile.

I also realized today that Linda and I have to break up. I realize now that her lack of imagination has been holding me back. She's been trying to mold me into someone I will never be. She's too somber, too materialistic, too straight. She thinks that life must be lived in the straight and narrow, but she's wrong and I learned that today. Today I learned that life is an adventure for people with courage.

I guess I should back up for a minute here. I don't really know where to start. I guess everything began when I dropped that acid Mike gave me for my birthday. When I got off, I decided to take a bath, and I was watching the water, just thinking about how beautiful it looked, how I've never really noticed how beautiful bathwater looked before, when out of nowhere I heard this incredible music, like chimes.

Eventually I realized that it was the front doorbell and then I thought, I better go answer it, you never know. And I stood up and realized that I was wet and naked and then I thought, Hey, so what? What difference does it make, really, in the grand scheme of things? So I went to the door and it was this girl from down the street who I have never met before, and I forgot what she wanted, but I invited her in and—this is the really strange part—she came in.

So there we were in my parents' living room and I'm naked and she's beautiful so I made some tea. It took me around an hour to do it. Then we just sat and talked about everything and I realized that I have this incredible power over people. Almost messianic. She sat there and listened with these big beautiful brown eyes. And then I kissed her. And we were kissing and I was naked and I had this erection and she looked at it and suddenly she said she had to leave.

And I said, "Why?" And then we met each other's eyes for a long time and she said because she realized that I was a very special person and that she didn't want to ruin a special moment with something as common as sex. And I understood deep down what she meant. I understood that she meant that we were connecting in a much deeper way, that it was all too much for right now.

And she left, and I started to think . . . that I must be the kind of man that women find irresistible, that I am special, that I have powers others don't have, and that I can't let myself be hindered. I must connect with everything in this world that wants me. So, I just lay down on the floor, naked, tripping, and I could feel the power moving through me, as if the whole world lay under me just to hold me up. I was literally on top of the world. I felt like GOD.

That was around five hours ago and I'm pretty straight now. After I write this down, I'm going to call Linda and tell her it's over between us. Then I'm going to wait for my parents and tell them I'm dropping out of Boston University. There's really no point to a liberal arts degree now, with all the potential I have within me. I've decided to take my savings, a thousand dollars, and move to Portland, Oregon, for a while. I think that will be a good place to begin.

Until tomorrow . . .

SHANTI

American Dreamer

A man stands in the middle of the stage. He knocks back an entire pint of wine in one swallow. He addresses passing cars.

Hey, bro! Hey, bro! bro! My MAN! How you doin' today? How you doin'?

I like dat car you're drivin', man . . . dat's a nice car. I like your car, man, I like your car. It's a nice car, man, how you doin' today? All right? ALL RIGHT!

I like your ol' lady sittin' dere too, man. HOW YOU DOIN', MAMA? Feelin' good? You're a beautiful lady, anybody ever tell you dat before? Bet he never tells you dat! (*Pulls his crotch.*)

How about you and me, we go aroun' da corner, drink a li'l bit more a dis T-Bird, I got a drop lef' here. How about it, whuddyousay? You and me gonna party all night. Come on, baby! Come on!

Huh?

Say what? Hey, watch your mouth, sucker. You don't know who you talkin' to. You don't know who you talkin' to. . . . Come over here and say dat, bro, come on, right now, come over here! Hey. Hey. Hey. I was jus' sayin' dat shit to her, make her feel better, man . . . 'cause she's stuck wid YOU! . . .

. . .

Huh? Get outa da car. I don't have to take dat shit from you! Come on, get out. . . .

Gowan back to New Jersey, wherever you come from, man. Go fill some teeth, whatever you do. Get outa here. . . . You think you such a big deal . . . wid your rusty ol' Cadillac. Huh! And your flea-bitten ol' lady. Ugly ol' lady.

I DON'T NEED YOUR OL' LADY! What do I need her for?

Shit! Huh! Shit!

What do I need your ol' lady for? Got me plenty a ol' ladies!

Man, I got me so many ol' ladies . . . had to buy me a whole 'partment building jus' to fill it up wid my ladies, man! I got ladies in ev'ry 'partment. Fashion models. Blondes, brunettes, redheads. Look like dey jus' come outa *Vogue* magazine . . .

. . . all sittin' aroun' in deir 'partments, polishin' deir nails, sittin' waitin' aroun', waitin' aroun' fo' ME, man! Dey get up in da mornin', dey say to demselves, "Where is he? Where is my MAN! When's he gonna come see me? I need my KISS!" Dat's what dey say!

And I'm up on da top, in da penthouse, smokin' a cigarette, eatin' some Doritos, watchin' Donahue. . . . I need me a lady, I want me a *taste*, a little *squeeze*. Shit! I got me an *intercom* system. I press on my intercom system: "BUUUUUUP!—Yo! Renetta, get your butt up here, I wanna *talk* to you!"

. . .

See what I'm sayin? I got ladies all day long . . . all day long. . . .

Don't need your car neither. Got me plenty a cars. Got me . . . shit . . . got me a whole parkin' garage full a cars down da bottom a my buildin'. . . . Got me Mercedes, Lamborghinis, Maseratis, Volares . . . all dem kind a cars. . . . Don't even drive 'em. Jus' look at 'em.

I wanna drive aroun' I got me a limousine, bro. Stretch limousine. Long stretch limousine. . . . Long, long, loooonng stretch limousine. Ladies like 'em long. I got a long one, man.

Got me a chauffeur . . . he hates me, takes him all day to buff down one side a da limousine . . . all day he polishes one side . . . next day, he goes down de other side, dat's how long it is!

Got me a TV set in my limousine . . . 'frigerator, swimmin' pool, bar . . . fully stocked bar in my limousine . . . wid whiskey, good whiskey: Ol' Crow, Ol' Grandad . . . all da good kind, da old kind . . . COLT 45 . . . ON TAP! . . . Perrier, dat Perrier shit. . . . Got it, don't drink it.

Got me toothpicks, napkins wid jokes on 'em, ice cubes . . . lil' plastic cups wid de chopped-up limes, chopped-up lemons, lil' red cherries . . . all dat shit. Got it. FRENCH WINE . . . from FRANCE!

(*He stumbles and falls to the floor.*)

I . . . I sit in da back a my limousine. . . . (*lies down*) . . . I lay down in da back a my limousine, I like dat even better. . . . I lay down . . . da ladies, dey all come down outa da building . . . lie on me in da back a da limousine . . . lie down next to me, lie down on top a me . . . piled up, stacked up, squishin' me flat. . . . HUGE pile a ladies like a bowl a Jell-O!

We drive aroun'. . . . Got me a hookah . . . smoke my hookah: opium, hashish, cheebah, all dat shit packed in my hookah dere. . . . I smoke it up. . . .

I get stoned . . . stoned . . . stoned outa my brain . . . and if I get too stoned out, I put my head back and da ladies dey sprinkle cocaine right down into my nostrils . . . jus' like dat! Right down dere. GOOD cocaine too. None a dat New Jersey dentist cocaine, man, I got da good kind . . . da kind da cops does, dat Miami cocaine . . . fill me right up, can't even breathe. . . .

Den I put out my arm . . . dey gimme de French wine . . . intravenously . . . right down dere in my arm. . . . Open up da sky roof, watch da clouds . . . da birds flyin' aroun' up dere. We drive aroun' . . . turn on da TV set, see what's on "Wheel a Fortune" dere, see how Vanna be doin' . . . drive aroun' wid my ladies, I say . . . Ohhhhhhhhhhhhhhhhh! Yeah!

Dat's what I do! I don't NEED your ol' lady. . . . Got my own thing goin' here, I got da American Dream, see, I do what I wanna do, I do what EVERYBODY wants to do. . . . I drive aroun' all day long . . . in my limousine. . . . I get high . . . put my head back . . . watch da clouds . . . and I . . . pass out . . . I pass out.

Wired

A sleepy man answers the phone in a nasal voice.

Yeah? Yeah. No, Arnie, you didn't wake me up. What time is it? Noon? (*Looks at watch*) It's nine o'clock in the morning, Arnie, what are you calling me nine o'clock in the morning for? Yeah, yeah, it's noon where you are, it's nine o'clock in the morning here. Yeah, no . . . no, Arnie, you're in New York, I'm in Los Angeles. It's noon where you are, it's . . . no I'm not gonna explain it to you. I'm up, I'm up, Arnie, I'm up. . . . Listen, will you hold . . . Arnie, Arnie, wait a minute. . . . Arnie, Arnie, hold, Arnie, hold . . . hold on for a second, lemme get a cup of coffee here. . . . I'll be righ—Arnie, hold on . . . lemme put you on hold. . . .

(*He puts the phone down, groggily sets up lines of coke . . . cuts it.*)

Arnie, you still there? Hold on. . . .

(*Snorts the coke.*)

Arnie? Lemme get the cream, hold on. . . .

(*Pulls out a bottle of bourbon from a cabinet, pours a triple shot, drinks it. . . . He shakes out his arms, rolls his shoulders. . . . He wakes up, talking very fast. He pauses briefly, only to listen.*)

Yeah Arnie, yeah, yeah, yeah. I'm here. I'm here. I'm here. I'm here, yeah, yeah, listen . . . listen . . . wait a minute, wait a minute . . . Arnie listen to me, will you listen to me? . . . You tell me how much money you got to spend, I'll tell you *who* you can get for your money. . . .

. . . Who? Lee Marvin?! Lee Marvin?! You're not talking Lee Marvin money here, Arnie. You're not talking Lee Marvin money, you're talking Bullwinkle the Moose money to me here. For the amount you're talking about, maybe, just maybe, and I'm not making any promises here, I can get you, I don't know . . . Robert Vaughn . . . Vince Edwards . . . not Lee Marvin. Forget about Lee Marvin, gimme another name. . . .

Who? Him? He's no good, he's a drug addict. He's a drug addict, Arnie . . . no, not that shit, the other thing. . . . YES! Yes, yes, yes . . . the hard stuff, yes, with the needles and the spoons and the forks and the knives and the whole routine. Yes. Arnie, this guy's idea of a good time is throwing up. You understand what I'm telling you? You're gonna find him in a bathroom someplace turning blue. He's dead meat. Forget about him. You don't want him. . . .

Huh? Of course it's a sad story, of course it's a sad story. . . . What's the guy, twenty-six, twenty-seven years old, he makes a million dollars a picture, he's a drug addict. . . . I should have his problems. . . . I'm crying my eyes out. My tears are running onto the receiver here. . . . FORGET ABOUT HIM! We'll go to his funeral. . . . Gimme another name. . . .

Who? . . . He's not available. He's got a broken hand. . . . He broke it working out. . . . He was working out on somebody's face, he broke his hand. . . . The guy called him a homosexual. So what if he's a homosexual? . . . He's a homosexual who likes to go around punching people in the face and breaking his hand. . . . Huh? . . . Yes, he's very macho. . . . Yes, he's very virile. . . . Yeah, he's got a great moustache. . . . Listen, Arnie, the macho man has a broken hand, OK? He couldn't punch out Ricky Schroeder today . . . . He's not available. Gimme another name.

Who else? . . . He's dead. . . . He's dead. He's literally dead. . . . He fell off his boat in Malibu, a shark ate him. Of course it's ironic, of course it's ironic, Arnie, what are you telling me ironic? They had to cancel the whole series. . . . Arnie, I would love to do the deal with you, I'm sorry the fish ate the guy . . . go talk to the shark. . . . HE'S DIGESTED, HE'S NOT AVAILABLE!

Arnie, hold on, I got another call coming in . . . hold on. . . . (*He punches the hold button.*)

Yeah? . . . SID, SID, SID, SID, SID, SID! Listen to me: YES! Do you hear me saying yes? I said yes. Yes. You have Richard Chamberlain. . . . Richard Chamberlain, *The Bhopal Story*, it's gonna happen. . . . Yes, *The Bhopal Story: The Tragic Story of a Misunderstood Multinational* starring Richard Chamberlain, name over the title, one hundred percent of the title, filmed on location in India with a cast of a thousand beggars. You're gonna make a million bucks on this thing, Sid. . . . Yes, you have the blind beggars . . . yes, you got the crippled beggars. . . . Will you get off my case, it's gonna be the greatest miniseries in the history of miniseries.

Huh? What do you mean you have some more people you want me to look at? Who? . . . Who's he? . . . The greatest actor in India? I never heard of him. . . . I never heard of him, Sid, I don't care if he's Mahatma Gandhi's grandson, if I never heard of him he's not coming in on this picture. . . . Because he's an unknown, that's why. . . . Why is he unknown? Because he doesn't have a name. . . . Sid, we're talkin' Richard Chamberlain here, OK? One of the greatest, if not the greatest, American actors of our time! I cannot have this great actor acting opposite some two-bit, unknown Hindu! I don't care if everyone in India has his face tattooed on their chests, he's an unknown in the States. . . . Wait a minute, wait a minute. . . . Sid, Sid, Sid, Sid, Sid . . . can I . . . can I . . . can I get a word in edgewise here for a second?

This guy, is he in the union? Is he in SAG? All right, listen, bring him down to the set, we'll give him some water to carry around, he can do a little Gunga Din routine for us there. . . . It's the best I can do, Sid. . . . Sid, I'm getting off the phone. . . . Have a nice time in India, watch out for the prime rib. . . . OK, yeah, ha ha. . . . (*Punches the hold button again.*)

Yeah, Arnie, I'm still here. . . .

Who? No I won't talk to him for you. Because he's insane, that's why. . . . Why is he insane? He's insane because he thinks he's God. . . . Have you talked to God lately, Arnie? Let me tell you something about "God." . . . He's an egomaniac. . . . And after a couple of drinks, he's a shitty actor too. . . .

Arnie, the man sits there on the set like Buddha . . . telling everybody what to do! He's telling the actors what to do, he's telling the director what to do, he's telling the lighting man what to do. . . . He's got an answer for everybody. . . . He's got the answer for everybody's problems. . . . you know what his answer to everybody's problems is? . . . HIS SCHLONG, that's what it is!

Fucking the girls? . . . He's fucking the girls, he's fucking the boys, he's fucking the stuntmen, you bend over in front of him, he'll be fucking you too, Arnie! . . . You'd like that, wouldn't you?

Listen, Arnie, the guy is a promiscuous egomaniac, he should be locked up in a padded cell. . . . I DON'T CARE HOW TALENTED HE IS! I DON'T CARE! . . . BECAUSE I HAVE MY PRINCIPLES. (*He drops to his knees and pounds the floor.*) Listen, Arnie, I'm gonna burst a blood vessel here in another second. . . . Just forget about him. . . .

Look, I can get you Lee . . . as a favor, he'll do it as a favor for me . . . uh, hundred thou. . . . Hundred thou—but only for five minutes. Arnie, I'm talkin' Lee Marvin here, one of the greatest if not the greatest American actor . . . that's it. . . . I don't want to talk about it, Arnie, if you're not gonna be rational . . . no . . . no . . . I'm getting off. . . . NO! I'm getting off, Arnie, hundred thou and that's 'cause you're my friend. . . . I love you too, Arnie, and from me that's a compliment. . . . Yeah. . . . Arnie, Arnie, Arnie. . . . Bye.

(*hangs up*)

Ceramic Tile

A man is standing, arms outstretched, holding a champagne bottle. He's talking in a Texas accent to someone, a girl.

Whoooeeee! I'm feelin' good tonight, I'm feelin' fine tonight. Come here, come here, come here, come darling . . . come on, come on, give Daddy, give Daddy a kiss . . . give me a kiss. . . . Come on. Come on. Come on. . . . Do ya love me? Do ya love me? Do ya love me? Sure ya do. . . . Come on, have some more champagne, here, darlin'. You gotta have yourself some more champagne! Come on. . . .

(*He gives a big whoozy kiss, and rocks on his heels.*)

YEAH? WHO IS IT? COME ON IN, DOOR'S UNLOCKED! . . . Yeah . . . just a, just, OK, just put it, bring it on into the room there, that's OK. Just put it over by the bed there, that'll be fine. Yeah. OK. Ummmm. Looks delicious. Yessir. Heh heh. All right. OK. Yeah. . . . Look, buddy, I'll sign for it later, give yourself five bucks, OK? Thank you too. All right. OK. All right. I will. OK. Heh heh. . . . Oysters do do that. . . . Yeah. Thanks a lot. Good night, buddy. Yeah, all right, I'm a little busy now so . . . all right. . . . OK. . . . Lock the door on your way out. . . . Thank you too. OK. All right. LOCK THE DOOR!

Where were we? Oh yeah, you gotta have some more of this good champagne here darling. You don't have some more champagne, I'm gonna have to drink it all myself! I drink it all myself, I'm gonna throw up all over your pretty party dress there. WHOOOOOEEEEEE! I'm feeling good tonight! I'm feelin' fine tonight.

(*coughs, slumps in a chair*)

Michelle. Michelle? . . . Michelle! See, I told you I'd remember your name!

Turn around for me a second, Michelle, lemme take a look at you. . . . Lemme take a look at you, go ahead, turn around. Yeah. . . . You're one hell of a good-looking girl, aren't you darlin'? You're just about the most beautiful girl I seen . . . the last twenty-four hours. You know that? You are.

You got beautiful breasts. You got a beautiful behind. You got everything right where it belongs and plenty of it, don't you, huh? (*drinks*) You can stop turning around now, Michelle.

How old you say you were?

Just a babe outa the woods, eh?

Guess. . . . Go ahead, guess. . . .

Forty-seven years old. My wife says I look like I'm sixty. She says being on the road all the time makes you get older faster. She thinks I enjoy being on the road. I hate being on the road. . . .

Tell you a secret. Tomorrow's my daughter's fourteenth birthday . . . and I can't be there. Can't be there at my own little girl's birthday party 'cause I gotta be here at this convention.

You know why I gotta be at this convention, Michelle? Because I am an industrial ceramic tile salesman. . . . And when you're an industrial ceramic tile salesman you gotta do one thing and you gotta do it real well. You gotta sell industrial ceramic tile. That's what I do, see, I sell tile. . . . I sell tile all the way from Tampa to San Diego. I sell tile and I sell a lot of it. I go to every little sales meeting, every convention, I go out there and bust my ass. . . .

It's a dog-eat-dog world out there, Michelle, and I go out there and I bite. . . . I bite as hard as I can and I don't let go 'til I make a sale. 'Cause I'm good. 'Cause I'm the best.

I work hard, Michelle. I work hard, you work hard. Everybody in the world works hard. Everybody in the whole world works hard . . . except my wife. My wife, my wife thinks money grows in checkbooks . . . she thinks her job is spending the money I earn. She thinks it's easy for me to go out there on the road, kill myself to bring back a couple of bucks so she can sit by the poolside flipping through her Saks Fifth Avenue catalogue picking out sterling-silver eggcups and fur-lined Cuisinarts. . . . She just sits there all day trying to figure out where to waste my money next. She thinks that's her job and . . .

What am I talking about her for when I'm here with you, right?

What do you do when you're not doing this, Michelle? Uh-huh. Good. You keep going to school. It's important to go to school. No future in this escort business, I'll tell you that. You keep going to school, Michelle, because . . . I want you to. You're a beautiful, sensitive girl and I wanna see good things happen to you, so you keep going to . . .

WHAT'S THAT LOOK? What's that look? I know, I know, I know what you're thinking. . . . I know what you're thinking. . . . You think I'm bullshitting you, don't you? You're looking at me you're thinking: here's another middle-aged, overweight, half-drunk . . . ceramic tile salesman. . . . I know, I know. . . . Well, let me tell you something, little girl, I may be middle-aged and I may be a little round at the edges and I may be feeling pretty good tonight . . . but I'm very different than the rest of these idiots you see here at this convention . . . don't confuse me with these salesmen guys.

I'm nothing like them, and I'll tell you why. . . . Because . . . see . . . I . . . you're looking at . . . you're in the same room with . . . the NUMBER ONE ceramic tile salesman in the United States of America. Numero uno. I sell more tile than all these guys put together. I sell more tile than anybody in the whole United States of America. . . . I probably sell more tile than anybody in the whole world!

Now think about that . . . that's a lot of tile. And I sell it all. Because I'm good, I'm the best, I'm special. And the reason why I'm special is . . . 'cause I care about people. I do. And I care about you, Michelle. Because you're special too. . . .

You know, tonight, when I came into the hotel, I thought to myself, I'm just gonna have a couple of drinks, go up to my room, pass out. But I saw you standing down there in the lobby, and I said to myself, "There is a beautiful, sensitive, intelligent, sophisticated girl . . . a beautiful girl with beautiful blue eyes . . . green eyes, beautiful green eyes . . . there's a girl I could talk to tonight." That's what I said to myself. There's a girl I can talk to.

Because I'll be honest with you, Michelle, I just need a little companionship. I'm just a lonely guy . . . just a lonely little cowboy. . . .

You know, every morning I wake up, I'm in a different hotel room . . . the first thing I hear is the alarm clock ringing by the bed, the first thing I see . . . the toilet . . . then I see the cable TV set down by the end of the bed . . . luggage on the floor, maid knockin' on the door, I got a headache and a hangover and I don't know where the hell I am!

Now if I don't know where I am, how the hell's anybody else supposed to know where I am? I feel like I'm the last man left in the whole world . . . and I get lonely, Michelle. . . . I get real lonely. . . .

Come here, come here, come here, baby, don't stand there all night, come here and give Daddy a hug. Come on.

Oh yeah . . . ummmm that's nice. . . .

SHIT! I'm jus' about gonna pass out on you here, Michelle! (*He slumps in his chair.*)

Lissen, Michelle, it was great talkin' to you, I want to tell you you're one hell of a stimulating conversationalist, you know . . . and I'll let you get out of here now . . . and I just want to tell you it was great . . . and uh . . . Michelle, before you go, though, uh . . . jus' so that hundred bucks don't go to a total waste, do you think you could do a little something for me right now . . . jus' so, jus' so your boss knows you're working? (*wink*) Huh? She tell you what I like, right? Think you could do a little bit of that for me right now? Huh? Just a quick one? Just a nice slow quick one?

Yeah, you got the idea . . . oh! Ummmmmmm. That's it. Yes. Oh, I feel better already. . . . Oh . . . I'll tell you something, Michelle . . . nothing worse . . . than being . . . lonely. . . .

Commercial

A man stands before a microphone. He holds a piece of paper in his hand. A voice speaks to him from a raspy loudspeaker.

VOICE: (*click*) What do you think, Eric? (*click*)

ERIC: Looks good. . . .

VOICE: (*click*) Yeah, uh . . . you wanna try it for me one time here, just throw something off? (*click*)

ERIC: We laid down more than one before. Which one did you like?

VOICE: (*click*) I'm sorry, what was that? (*click*)

ERIC: We did more than one take, which one did you like?

VOICE: (*click*) Uh . . . I think we liked the third one. (*click*)

ERIC: Warm?

VOICE: (*click*) Macho. But with a smile. You're selling virility. (*click*)

ERIC: Gotcha. I think I can do that.

VOICE: (*click*) Good . . . uh, you wanna give Jimmy a level? (*click*)

ERIC: Sure. (*reading*) Krönenbräu. Krönenbräu. Krönenbräu. Krönenbräu. Krönenbräu. Krönen—

VOICE (*cutting in*): (*click*) That's fine. OK. So, uh, let's try it once, OK? (*click*)

ERIC: I'm ready.

VOICE: (*click*) Remember, Eric, this is the voice inside your head. The guy wants to get laid and you've got the secret. (*click*)

ERIC: Wants-to-be-part-of-the-crowd kind of guy.

VOICE: (*click*) Right. OK? Jimmy will give you the cue. No slate. (*click*)

ERIC: You've worked hard to get . . . I'm sorry, can we start over again? I'm not . . . concentrating. . . .

VOICE: (*click*) OK. We're still running. (*click*)

ERIC: You've worked hard to get where you are today and you've still got a long way to go before you get to the top. . . . You want your life to be *good* . . . so you surround yourself with the best . . . the very best . . . in clothes, in food, in people. . . . You know you're going to get there someday . . . and when you do, you'll say "good-bye" to your companions of a less prosperous time. But there is one thing you will never leave behind. . . .

And that's your beer: Krönenbräu . . . always superb, always fulfilling, always the best . . . because you're the best. . . .
Just taste it and feel its *strength* fill you. . . .
Ahhhh. . . . Krönenbräu. The thing you have before everything else. Krönenbräu. The beer of kings.

VOICE: (*click*) OK, Eric, sounds good. Nice and warm, but macho, I'll buy it. . . . Just gimme the tag three times, OK? and then we'll uh . . . play it back. I think we'll be all done for the day. . . . I think that's all right. . . . We're gonna, we're gonna keep it. . . . (*click*)

ERIC: That's it? Great. OK, tag three times:

(*clears throat*)

(*normal voice*) Ahhhhhh. . . . Krönenbräu. The thing you have before everything else. Krönenbräu. The beer of kings.
(*peppy voice*) Ahhhhhh. . . . Krönenbräu. The thing you have before everything else. Krönenbräu. The beer of kings.
(*deep voice*) Ahhhhh. . . . Krönenbräu. The thing you have before everything else. Krönenbräu. The beer of kings.

(*looks up for approval, fade out*)

Melting Pot

A man in a V-neck T-shirt stands and gesticulates with his arms, shouting with a Greek accent.

LISA! LISA! Get this guy over here. . . . What do you want? What do you want? Huh? Cup of coffee? What else? That's it, cup of coffee? . . . LISA, get this bum cup of coffee. . . .

Where the hell is Jesus? (*shouts at the floor*) JESUS! JESUS! What are you doing down there? . . . Shooting up? Jerking off? Come on, come out of there. . . . What rat? . . . Leave the rat, if it's dead leave it. . . . Come up here now, come on, come here, I want to show you something.

OK, come here. . . . What is this? Huh? What is this mess? French fries in the fat, french fries on the floor, french fries in the sink, everyplace french fries. Mess, mess, mess, mess, mess, mess. Eh? Huh? Look at me when I'm talking to you! Look at me. Don't look at girl over there, look at me. . . .

Who teach you to make mess like this? I don't teach you to make mess. You want Health Department come in here, they close us up, they say, "George too dirty, close up!"?

I show you how to make french fries, you don't make no more mess, all right. . . .

Yeah, yeah, yeah, yeah, yeah. . . . I know you know, I know you know, you know everything, you genius! . . . George show you how to make french fries, no more mistake, all right? No more messy. Yeah, yeah, you watch me, mister. . . .

. . .

Take bag, all right, cut corner on bag, all right? Yeah, I know you know, smart guy. . . . Einstein, you watch me. Take bag, put in basket, all right? (*His arms flail wildly*.)

In . . . in . . . not all over . . . in the basket. One shake. Put back, take basket, put in fat, all right? Cooking. . . . Cooking. . . . Cooking. . . . Easy, nothing to it! . . . Cooking. . . . Cooking. . . .

Then shake, shake, bim, bim, boom, boom, zip, zip! Back in. Cooking. . . . Cooking. . . . Cooking. . . . All right, take it out . . . brown, white, don't make no difference, nobody eat it anyway. . . .

All right, now you show me. Show me, I want to see, come on. I don't got all day here, please, I'm busy. . . .

(*watching*) All right, OK, yaaaaa, ummmmm, all right, put it in, ummmmm, yaaaaaa, OK.

You know, I don't have to hire you, you know. Lisa, she tell me you good.

That Chinese guy, he was great! Buck an hour that guy, huh? . . . Too bad he die on me. . . .

Come on, come on, put it back now, you're spilling, you're spilling! . . .

You know what your problem is, Jesus? You Puerto Rican. You go back whenever you want to go back. You come, you go, you don't need green card, you be citizen when you want be citizen. I can't go back. I have to stay in America.

You want to stay in America, you have to work all the time. . . .

I want to be big success in America. I work sometimes twenty-four hours a day, I work. Sometimes I don't eat, I don't sleep, I don't piss. Nothing. Working all the time. That's it. You know what I'm saying?

You don't work all the time, you know what's gonna happen to you? You gonna be like all these these these bums, these junkies, these winos . . . they come in here, they hang around all the time, night and day. "Gimme cup a coffee. Gimme cup a coffee. Gimme glass a water—I wanna shoot up. I wanna throw up! Cup a coffee. Glass a water. Cup a coffee. Glass a water. . . ."

You want cup a coffee? You want glass a water? You go back to Puerto Rico. They got water there, they got coffee, all day long. You want to be in America, you work. That's it. Working all the time. All right? That's it. Work.

No time for this . . . wine . . . this drugs . . . this hanging around, pinball, disco, girlfriends, TV, movies . . . bullshit.

(*pounds chest*) WORK! WORK! WORK! WORK! WORK!

You work, you make money, you buy house . . . you go in melting pot, you melt. That's the American way. You know what I'm saying? Think about these things. All right. All right.

Come on, OK, that's good. A little burn, but OK. All right, that be your lunch today. . . . Double order french fries.

Is good for you. Lots of vitamins. . . . (*pats Jesus on the back*)

Don't worry. Don't worry. Don't cry. You learn how to make french fries, don't worry . . . two, three years you make as good as George. Good boy.

LISA! LISA! Take over for me, I'm going to the bank, I gotta make a deposit. . . .

(*walks off*)

Our Gang

A tough guy, holding a beer bottle, T-shirt sleeves rolled up, struts onstage.

(*turning*) Tony, you goin' to the store? Get me a pack a cigarettes, will ya? Marlboro . . . hard pack. And get me a Ring-Ding too, I'm hungry. . . . Get me a Diet Pepsi too, I'm starved, didn' have no breakfast or nothin'. . . . Please? Please? Come on man, I got a hangover man, I'm disabled. I'll pay ya back later. . . . Yer a saint man. . . .

(*turning and sipping his beer*) I'm all right. . . . I'm all right. . . . Where were you last night, Joe? We was lookin' all over the place for you. It was FUCKIN' GREAT man! You missed the whole fuckin' thing. Me and Frankie and Sally and Joanie, we had these 'ludes, Frankie got 'em outa the drugstore where he works. . . . So we took these 'ludes, I figure let's take the 'ludes, take my car, drive up the highway, smoke a couple a "j's," drink a couple a beers, listen to some Bruce on the radio, you know, make a quiet night of it, stay outa trouble, right? Right.

So we're drivin' around, I'm not gettin' off on the 'ludes, right? So I turns to Frankie, I says, "Frankie, I'm not gettin' off on these 'ludes." Frankie turns to me, he says, "Don't worry man, you will. . . ." You know with that, like, wisdom that Frankie's got, he just knows stuff. . . .

So I'm drivin', I'm drivin', waitin' for the 'ludes to kick in and I looks down and I see I got this little piece a dirt on my shoe. And you know me, I'm neat and clean, I don't like gettin' nothin' on my clothes or nothin'. So I'm drivin', I keep lookin' down at this piece a dirt . . . piece a dirt's drivin' me crazy. It's like me and this piece a dirt we got this thing goin' on here between us. . . . I'm lookin' down I keep seein' this piece a dirt. It's lookin' at me, I'm lookin' at it. Back and forth, drivin' me nuts. I'm mesmerized by the dirt. So, I start scratchin' the dirt off my shoe. . . . I'm scratchin', I'm scratchin'. . . . Got my hand on the wheel, drivin' the car, not fuckin' aroun' or nothin'.

Scratchin', scratchin' . . . all of a sudden . . . out a fuckin' noplace: BANG! This guardrail comes up the front a the car! Car starts turnin' aroun', chicks is screamin' in the backseat, cars honkin' their horns all around me and shit. . . . BOOM! We go over the guardrail, we're on the other side of the highway now, goin' down the highway . . . cars blinkin' their headlights at me and shit . . . you know, like I don't know I'm on the wrong side of the road!? People are so stupid! BANG! We go down the side of the road, into this you know, valley-gully thing, down by the side of the road. ZING! Car comes to a stop.

I gets outa the car. Frankie gets outa the car. Sally gets outa the car. Joanie gets outa . . . everybody gets outa the car. Everybody's cool, everybody's fine, everybody's healthy, right? Great. . . . The car, Joe. You had to see the car, man. It was great. Everything was gone from the outside of the car, you know? The bumpers was gone, and the headlights was gone, and the handles was gone and the license plate . . . the car was one big scrape. It looked like, it looked like . . . you know E.T.? Little fuckin' E.T.? It looked like fuckin' E.T.'s head. (*laughs*)

Frankie comes . . . Frankie comes over to the car, he comes over. He looks at the car like this, he says, "Fuck the fuckin' car, man, the fuckin' car's fucked!" Right? (*laughs*) With that razor wit of his, you know, *zing*! The guy's a fuckin' wordmaster . . . thinkin' all the time. . . .

All right, so I figure, let's ditch the car, we're holdin' 'ludes, let's get outa here before the cops show . . . so we start hitchin' down the highway. . . .

Nobody's pickin' us up. . . . I don't know why. . . . Joanie's just got a little blood runnin' down her face, that's it. Nothin'. So we're standin' there, finally, this van shows up. Big peace sign painted on the side, flowers painted . . . yeah, yeah, that's it, a hippie van, like outa prehistoric times. . . . Door pops open, guy drivin' the van, Joe, you had ta see this guy. He's got hair down to his butt, he's got a headband on, incense, flowers, beads, Grateful Dead music on the tape player, you know, complete asshole. . . .

We figure, what the hell, why not? So we all jumps inside this guy's van. Joanie gets in the front seat, the rest of us gets in the backseat. We start drivin'.

Joe. The guy starts rollin' these joints. You had to see these joints, they were huge, the size of ya dick. No, even bigger, the size of MY dick, enormous! (*laughs*) Monster joints, made outa some kind of weed, I never smoked weed like this before in my life. The strongest weed I ever smoked. Like from one of those weird oriental places, like Taiwan. . . . Taiwan weed, that's what it was. Taiwan weed, all right. . . . Smoke one toke a this shit, ya blind for the rest of ya life! Good weed, strong weed.

Me and Frankie, we each roll up a monster joint of this stuff and we're in the backseat, blowin' smoke rings around each other's head. Like getting completely wasted, just wasted outa our brains, vaporized. Meltin'-into-the-upholstery kind of thing . . . oxygen-tent time, you know? We're doin' experiments on our brain cells . . . like how many can you kill in one toke? (*laughs*)

Totally, totally screwed into the fuckin' ground, blown inside out, comatose, right? Even the Grateful Dead music's startin' ta sound good. . . . "Truckin' with da Doo-Dah Man!" (*laughs, then starts coughing*) Blasted! Then . . . then the 'ludes kick in!

All right. Now, check this out. Party time, right? OK. So we're drivin' along, havin' this good time, and all of a sudden this guy, this hippie guy, he reaches over, he puts his hand on Joanie's leg! Frankie's sittin' in the backseat, he goes like, "Hey, man, take ya hand off my girlfriend's leg!" Right?

The guy turns around to Frankie, he says: "Hey, man . . . (*shoots his middle finger*) . . . fuck you!" Right? To Frankie he says this. . . .

So what's Frankie gonna do? He takes his knife out, he opens it up, he goes: "No, man, *fuck you*!" Right?

The guy reaches into the glove compartment, pulls out a handgun, points it at Frankie's head, he says: "No, man, FUCK YOU!"

I'm fuckin' shittin' my pants, right, 'cause you do not fuckin' fuck with Frankie! . . . You know what I'm talkin' about? We're in a movin' vehicle here, we've got a loaded gun here, I'm not feelin' good about this. . . .

. . .

Frankie's sittin' there like a stick a dynamite, just vibratin', right? The guy turns around ta look at the road for one second, Frankie takes the knife, *bing*! Cuts the guy behind the ear. . . . Little tiny cut, nothin' cut, hardly bleedin'.

Guy gets pissed off. Pulls the van to the side of the road. Says, "Everybody outa the van right now!" The van's stopped by the side of the road. He's wavin' the gun around in front a Frankie's face. . . .

What's Frankie gonna do? He takes his knife, closes it up nice. . . . (*punches*) BANG! BANG! BANG! BANG! BANG! BANG! BANG! The guy's head. . . . (*kicks*) BOOM! BOOM! BOOM! BOOM! BOOM! BOOM! Kicks the guy outa the van. WHAM! WHAM! WHAM! WHAM! WHAM! WHAM! In the ribs, guy's on the ground. Frankie just bends over, picks up the gun, gets back in the van, we're outa there. FRANKIE!!! (*laughing*)

We leave the guy in the middle of the highway lookin' like the Woodstock revolution or somethin'. "GET A HAIR-CUT, HIPPIE!" (*laughing*)

So now we got the guy's van. . . . So Frankie's drivin', he takes the van down off the highway, so no cops, right? There's a little road down into these woods. Frankie's drivin' . . . real careful: "Oh, there's a tree!" BANG! "Oh, there's another tree!" CRASH! "There's a rock!" BOOM! Beatin' the hell outa this guy's van. . . . CRACK! We break the axle. . . .

. . .

We're in the middle of the woods, we don't know where we are. . . . Frankie gets outa the van, he looks at the axle, he goes: "Don't worry, man, I can fix it!"

He gets in the back of the van, he looks around, finds a can of gasoline and starts splashin' the gasoline all over the inside of the van. . . . He turns to me, he says, "Richie, can I see ya cigarette fa a second?" I couldn't figure out what he wants my cigarette for. . . . He takes one puff outa my cigarette, flips it in the van. . . .

BOOM! The van blows up! Joe, you had to see this thing, man, it was nice, man. It was really nice. . . . Fireball, ten, fifteen feet high . . . like this . . . colors in it and everything. It was beautiful, one of the most beautiful things I ever seen. . . .

Plus we's in the woods, right? You ever been in the woods before, real woods? Nice in the woods. . . . Not like Central Park. . . .

This fireball's burnin' like this in the middle of the woods, and we're in this clearin' and all around us you got like . . . trees, you know, with leaves on 'em and stuff, and like the flames, they're like reflectin' up on the leaves, you know. Then up over ya head, ya got like stars . . . and it's quiet, ya know, real quiet in the woods. You don't hear nothin' . . . just, like, maybe a headlight poppin' or the windshield wipers meltin' onto the hood . . . nice, you know, quiet. . . .

And I'm just standin' there, the fire's burnin', the stars, the 'ludes, my friends standin' next ta me . . . it was like spiritual or somethin'. I never felt so calm in my life. . . .

Joanie was lookin' in the flames, she said she could see Jim Morrison's face like floatin' in there.

Frankie's totally into it. Frankie's spiritual, you know. Ever talk to Frankie about Satan? He knows all about Satan.

He turns to me, he goes like this, he goes, "Here man, take this."

I says, "Frankie, I can't take any more shit, I'm gonna fall down!"

He says, "Take it, man, take it. Trust me, it'll wake you up. . . ."

So I takes the stuff, I figures it's crystal or speed or pep pills, somethin' harmless like that . . . it's triple-strength LSD! Acid, we're doin' acid. I haven't done acid for at least three . . . weeks. . . .

ZOOOOOOM! Everything's meltin' and weird and stuff. . . . Plus it's the woods, so you got trees and rocks and crazy shit like that, right? Not like in the city where everything's nice, easy to figure out. . . . You're walkin' along, smashed outa ya brains . . . a little squirrel runs out . . . looks like a fuckin' rhinoceros! (*He jumps.*)

And Frankie, he's still got the guy's gun, right? So he's walkin' along. . . . BANG, BANG, BANG, BANG, BANG!

Shootin' in the air, trying to see how far up the bullet goes. . . .

Anyways, to make a long story short, we ends up comin' to this big field. . . . Beautiful field with like a beautiful farmhouse in the middle of it, the kind of farmhouse, like, the Pepperidge Farm guy, he'd live in that farmhouse, right? Nice farmhouse. . . .

Frankie says: "Check this out. He goes up to the farmhouse . . . (*laughing*) . . . he's such a practical joker . . . goes right up to the front door . . . doo-doo-doo-doo-doo . . . rings the doorbell and this little old lady comes to the front door. And like, Frankie, he takes the gun, he goes . . . he goes like this: "Helter skelter, run fa shelter, let us in!"

(*laughing*) We go waltzing into these people's house, we're like completely bonked outa our brains, we don't know where we are or nothin'.

This old guy's like comin' down the stairs puttin' on his bathrobe, doin' this like, you know, "What's goin' on down here?" kind of thing, right? "Can I help you boys?" He's tryin' to threaten us or somethin', right?

Frankie takes the gun, he wasn't gonna hurt the guy or nothin', he just takes the gun goofin' aroun', takes the gun and goes up to the old guy like this, he goes (*pointing his finger*): "Say one more word, Grampa, I'll blow ya brains all over the wallpaper!" (*laughing*) "Blow ya brains all over the wallpaper?" Where does Frankie think this shit up? He's so funny!

. . .

Anyways, we gets the guy and the old lady, we put 'em on the floor, we cut their phone wires, tie 'em up with the phone wire, like on *Kojak*. Frankie's still into it. He's standin' over them with the gun: "We're the Charles Manson gang. If you tell anybody about us, we're gonna come back and burn ya house down!" I'm like, "Come on, Frankie, time to get outa here, man. You don't want to give these people the wrong impression about us or nothin'. Enough's enough!"

So anyway, we take their car keys, we take some booze, we hightail it outa there over ta Frankie's father's house. It's like four o'clock in the morning or somethin'. . . .

Huh?

Nah, his dad ain't home at four in the morning! His dad's an alcoholic, man, he's on the street all night drinking his face off. You ever meet his dad? . . . Aw, yeah, it's pathetic, he's got like a beer in one hand and a whiskey in the other. Yeah, I feel bad for Frankie, his father's so fucked up.

Anyway, so we like got the stereo on full-blast, we're dancin', we're partyin', me and Frankie and everybody, we're havin' a great time. . . . Joanie's in the bathroom throwin' up, 'cause she's got lousy tolerance. Couple a 'ludes, acid, it goes to her head.

OK. Now Sally starts comin' on to me, right? I been tryin' to make this chick for three months or somethin' and now she's standin' in front a me doin' this like, "Richie, Richie, I really want to go home with you, I need you, I want you. I love you. Take me home right now . . . uh-uh-uh-uh-uh!" Like this, right?

I'm standin' there, I'm lookin' at her thinkin' to myself: She's beautiful . . . she's stoned . . . she don't know what she's sayin' . . . her eyes aren't even open, fah cryin' out loud. (*pause*) What the hell, go for it!"

So I take the car keys, I start drivin' her home. . . . She's hot! She's got her hands down my pants, she's got her tongue in my ear, she's drivin' me crazy. . . .

I'm drivin' as fast as I can . . . six, seven miles an hour at least. (*laughs*)

I finally get to in front of her parents' house and when I turns to her to like start romanticizing her and shit, you know, I turns and . . . she's passed out! She's on the floor, curled up in a ball under the glove compartment, she's under there. . . .

So what am I gonna do? I'm a gentleman, I don't mess with unconscious broads. . . . So I gets outa the car, I go around, I pulls her outa the car. . . .

I brings her up to the front door of her parents' house and her parents they got like a regular front door and they got a screen door, you know? So I opens up the screen door, and I like wedge her up between the two doors . . . lock the door, ring the doorbell . . . get the hell outa there!

(*laughs, slaps hands with Joe*)

(*unzips his fly, turns his back to the audience, looks down*)

. . .

So anyways, listen, Joe, we're goin' out again tonight man, you should come along with us. . . . It's a lot of fun. . . . You know, it'd be a good time, Frankie likes you and everything. . . . (*zipping up*) Oh, yeah, Frankie wanted me to ask you one thing . . . uh (*adjusts his cock in his pantleg*) . . . you got a car?

No Problems

A man comes out to center stage and in a normal voice casually addresses the audience.

I have no problems. I'm happy with life. Things are fine as far as I'm concerned. I know some people have problems, some people have quite a few. I, fortunately, have none.

First of all, I'm in perfect health. I just got back from the doctor's office, he gave me a completely clean bill of health. He checked me from top to bottom. He couldn't believe what great shape I'm in. I guess all that jogging and bran paid off. He even checked my teeth . . . no cavities . . . so I'm in perfect health.

I have a good job. It's a, uh . . . I guess you would call it a "semicreative" job, very little pressure to perform. I put in about forty hours a week . . . when I want to. I have the weekends off every week, three weeks' paid vacation in the summer. I get paid very well for what I do. It's a good job. I like it.

My wife and I have been married fifteen years. We're very loving and have a very supportive relationship. My wife's a very attractive, a very lovely lady. We have a great sex life, if you have to know. I don't fool around. Wasn't it Paul Newman who said, "Why go out for hamburger when you can have steak at home?" I subscribe to that theory.

Our daughter's eleven and she's doing very well in school. She gets very high grades, has a lot of friends. Besides her school work she also uh . . . she's also studying modern dance, violin. Next month she starts her Latin lessons. She's a very precocious, very pretty little girl. We like her very much.

Our parents are alive on both sides and uh . . . we all like each other. None of this "mother-in-law" stuff in our household. We all enjoy each other's company. They're all retired now. They worked hard and saved during their active years and now they're enjoying a . . . "golden harvest" so to speak. Certainly no burden on us, we're very proud of them.

Our friends are all happy and healthy as far as we know. We usually see them around once a week. We go over to their house and uh . . . have dinner over at their house. Or at our house. I like to cook. I'm kind of a gourmet chef. I like to cook things like uh . . . I don't know . . . uh, tortellini with sun-dried tomatoes or uh . . . arugula salad with endives, something you wouldn't think of . . . that's my cooking style. Or we go out and see a movie . . . something with Meryl Streep in it or . . . uh, a play, a Sam Shepard play usually or one of those one-person shows or magic or juggling plays. We like them, there's so many to choose from. . . . Or we go bowling. We all like to bowl. They're very nice people, we've had a lot of good times with them.

So that's it, uh . . . our neighborhood is safe and clean. We have an excellent town council, an activist school committee (and that's important!). Ummm . . . fire department, police department, garbage disposal . . . all top-rated.

. . .

The house is in good shape, just had a new boiler put in last year, there's nothing wrong with the house. The Volvo's running smoothly, nothing wrong with the car. So uh. . . .

I mean, there are times when, uh, I mean, I'll be honest . . . there are times when I am concerned about all the, uh, you know, all the trouble there is in the world these days. You know, you turn on the news and uh . . . it's disturbing, you know . . . and nobody likes being disturbed. I make myself watch it because I know I should. For their sake.

And I worry about it all. But then I just think to myself, There's always been trouble, we didn't invent it, you know, and uh, I should just be thankful for all the good things I have in my life. Those people are doing their thing out there, whatever it is and uh, well anyway, I . . . I guess this isn't really the point. . . .

The future looks good. We're going to have the house paid off in ten years. We're buying a little condo down by the water, kind of as an investment/vacation/retirement thing. We're really excited about that. . . .

Ummmm, we've got money in a pension fund, so we're cool there . . . insurance . . . some stock.

Like I said, I have no problems. None. I'm happy. I'm healthy. I love my wife, I love my kid . . . good job . . . no problems.

That's what it's all about . . . I guess.

Godhead

A strip of white light falls across a man seated in pitch-black, holding a microphone. He speaks slowly in a guttural voice.

The way I see it, it's a fucked-up world, it's not going anyplace, nothing good is happening to nobody, you think about it these days and nothing good is happening to anybody and if something good is happening to anybody, it's not happening to me, it's not happening to myself.

The way I see it, there be this man, some man sitting in a chair behind a desk in a room somewhere down in Washington, D.C. See, and this man, he be sitting there, he be thinking about what we should do about crime rate, air pollution, space race. . . . Whatever this guy supposed to be thinking about. And this guy, he be sitting down there and thinking, and he be thinking about what's happenin' in MY life . . . he be deciding on food stamps, and work programs, and the welfare, and the medical aid and the hospitals, whether I be working today. Makin' all kinds a decisions for me. He be worrying about how I spen' my time! Then he lean back in his ol' leather chair, he start thinkin' about da nukular bomb. He be deciding whether I live or die today! Nobody makes those decisions for me. That's for me to decide. I decide when I want to get up in da mornin', when I want to work, when I want to play, when I want to do shit! That's my decision. I'm free. When I die, that's up to God or somebody, not some guy sittin' in a chair. See?

I just wanna live my life. I don't hurt nobody. I turn on the TV set, I see the way everybody be livin'. With their swimming pools and their cars and houses and living room with the fireplace in the living room. . . . There's a fire burnin' in the fireplace, a rug in front of the fireplace. Lady. She be lyin' on the rug, evenin' gown on . . . jewelry, sippin' a glass o' cognac. . . . She be lookin' in the fire, watchin' the branches burnin' up . . . thinkin' about things. Thinkin'. Thinkin'. What's she thinkin' about?

I jus' wanna live my life. I don't ask for too much. I got my room . . . got my bed . . . my chair, my TV set . . . my needle, my spoon, I'm OK, see? I'm OK.

I get up in the mornin' I combs my hair, I wash my face. I go out. I hustle me up a couple a bags a D . . . new works if I can find it.

I take it back to my room, I take that hairwon. I cook it up good in the spoon there. . . . I fill my needle up.

Then I tie my arm (*caressing his arm*) . . . I use a necktie, it's a pretty necktie, my daughter gave it to me. . . . Tie it tight . . . pump my arm . . . then I take the needle, I stick it up into my arm . . . find the hit . . . blood. . . .

Then I undoes the tie . . . I push down on that needle . . . and I got everything any man ever had in the history of this world. Jus' sittin' in my chair. . . .

(*voice lower*) I got love and I got blood. That's all you need. I can feel that blood all going up behind my knees, into my stomach, in my mouth I can taste it. . . . Sometimes it goes back down my arm, come out the hole . . . stain my shirt. . . .

. . .

I know . . . I know there's people who can't handle it. Maybe I can't handle it. Maybe I'm gonna get all strung out and fucked up. . . .

. . . . Even if I get all strung out and fucked up, don't make no difference to me. . . . Even I get that hepatitis and the broken veins and the ulcers on my arms . . . addicted. Don't make no difference to me. I was all strung out and fucked up in the first place. . . .

Life is a monkey on my back. You ride aroun' in your car, swim in your warm swimming pool. Watch the fire . . . I don't mind. I don't mind at all. Just let me have my taste. Have my peace. Just leave me be. Just leave me be.

(*turns in toward the dark*)

The Law

A man walks the stage with a microphone, addressing the audience. He's some sort of preacher.

What has happened to our country? Will somebody answer that question for me, please? We are in trouble. We are in serious trouble. Look around you, what do you see? Crime, perversion, decay, apathy. We are living in a nightmare.

You can't walk down the street for fear of being assaulted. You can't ride in an airplane for fear of being hijacked or blown up. Every corner newsstand openly sells vicious pornography. Every doctor's office is perfectly happy to perform an abortion on you . . . or your daughter. . . . Our children! Our children are subjected daily to the perversions of their schoolteachers and when they come home from school they have nothing better to do than to take drugs or alcohol, watch television, learn how to become homosexuals and rapists. . . .

What a lovely situation, is it not? It is the world we live in today.

In the Bible . . . they tell us of two cities. The worst cities that God had ever seen. They did everything in these cities. They committed every act, natural and unnatural. . . . And God, He looked down on these cities . . . and He saw sin. And He destroyed these cities.

Now you know what cities I'm talkin' about! I'm talkin', of course, about the cities of Sodom and Gomorrah . . . and friends, I regret to inform all of you here tonight . . . that everything they did in those cities of Sodom and Gomorrah . . . they do today . . . they do today. And more. And God destroyed those cities. . . .

Now friends, we have to be honest with ourselves, we have to ask ourselves: "From whence have come these plagues?" And isn't the answer right before our eyes? Do you really have to go to the fountainhead and tell me that the water is poisoned? Well, if you do, go ahead . . . go into the inner cities. Take a look at the Negroes and the Latins congregating on every street corner. . . . Take a look at the homos and dykes openly strutting up and down the avenues. . . . Take a look at the pimps and prostitutes and the junkies, conspiring with the Jewish slumlords, the Arab bankers and the Italian Mafioso . . . cutting this country up and destroying it piece by piece!

Don't look to the churches to save you! Don't look to the government to save you! Don't look to the corporations to save you! There's only one place to look for salvation, friends, and that's within yourselves. . . . In your hearts! In your hearts, you know the truth. In your hearts, that's where God is! God's inside your heart, He's a little voice inside you.

When you walk down the street and you see something terrible, you can't believe it and you think to yourself: What a horrible thing! That's the voice of God inside you. When you see something and you think to yourself: How can I stop this? What can I do to stop this? I have to stop this, I have to stop this now! That's the voice of God inside you. I know you have this voice. . . . I know you feel it. . . .

We can feel it, we can ALL feel it . . . deep inside . . . burning . . . the truth is burning. . . .

Just as it burned in the heart of Bernie Goetz when he took out that handgun and shot down those Negro subway criminals, he knew the truth. He knew that we are in a war for our souls! . . . And he who will not protect what is his . . . is condemned to lose it!

We must continue to put pressure on these Satanic abortion clinics, on these Negro subway criminals, on these Jewish media personalities like Alan Berg, who only understand the discipline of the bullet. These pornographers, like Larry Flynt, who only understand the discipline of the bullet. These homosexual politicians, like Harvey Milk, who only understand the discipline of the bullet. We must show them, we must teach them. God needs our help!

(*He looks the audience in the eyes.*) These people . . . these people . . . these people have sold their souls to the Devil . . . and if you don't believe me, you go down to Skid Row, take a look at the fallen bodies of the hopeless lost souls, their outstretched filthy hands still trying to reach out and pick up that empty wine bottle! This is the Devil's work right there for you to see! Go down to the red-light district, take a look at some of that porno, take a look at some of those magazines with the young girls on the cover, showing what they should never show anybody, the Devil dancin' in their eyes . . . these girls are lost! Go down to the city morgue, have 'em show you the dead bodies of the junkies, cold and stiff, lost and forgotten, lying on those metal tables. . . . These people have no souls. . . .

. . .

You go down to the city hospital, you have them show you the AIDS ward . . . go ahead and take a look . . . take a good look . . . and tell me what you see. . . .

This is Satan's work! This is the work of the Devil. The Devil is in the world today! He's sittin' here with us right now. He's sittin' here, and he's laughin'. He's laughin' at us because he seduced us with a life of plenty and he invited us into Hell.

And we all went, didn't we? We took him up on it, didn't we? And we're all goin' down to Hell. . . . You're goin' and you're goin' and you and you! And your children are goin' and your children's babies.

As the blind lead the blind, as the damned lead the damned, onward into oblivion we're goin'. We're goin' down to Hell, unless we do what we know is right! Unless we do what God wants us to do! Unless we do what that little voice inside tells us to do!

If you have to take a bottle, fill it up with gasoline, light it on fire, throw it into one of these abortion clinics, then you do it! If you have to take a handgun, load it up, shoot down one of these black urban barbarians, then you do it! If you have to take a nuclear device and cast it into some country filled with nothing but bearded, terrorist heathens, then you do it.

You do what you have to do! You do what you know is right.

Because this is the world where Satan walks, where Satan walks and where Satan laughs. . . . Where Satan says to himself: "I WON. I BEAT 'EM. I BEAT 'EM ALL."

There's a few of us who don't agree with Mister Satan. There's a few of us who are going to do everything we can, everything within our power . . . to stop him, to do the Lord's work . . . and make America, and hopefully the rest of the world . . . free of sin . . . again.

Are you with us? Thank you. Amen.

Master of Ceremonies

A man holding a microphone speaks in a highly modulated "DJ" voice.

Thank you, thank you, thank you. . . . I'm Ricky Rocket from WXXX . . . and you all know why we're here, you all know what tonight is all about: the last of the Krönenbräu Music Concerts series. And we've saved the best for last! Direct from England, the heaviest of the heavies, more metal to melt your mind: The Molesters! They're gonna come out in just a little while. They're in the back now, strappin' on the leather, strappin' on the metal, polishing their weapons and powdering their noses. They're gonna come out and they're gonna *take you down*. But before they do . . . one of my favorite bands, one of the hardest-rockin' bands ever to kick ass this side of Nagasaki. Direct from New Jersey . . . Satan Teens! Ya! Singing their new hit number one this week: "Die Young Die Happy"! They're gonna come out and they're gonna kick your teeth down your throat. But before they do . . . a band you have to see to believe, a band that makes going to the dentist feel like a party, a band, we don't even know where they come from: Cerebral Hemorrhage! Ya. They're gonna come out and they're gonna blow your mind right out of your skull! TONIGHT! LIVE ON THIS STAGE, CEREBRAL HEMORRHAGE, SATAN TEENS AND THE MOLESTERS ARE GOING TO ROCK YOU 'TIL YOUR NOSE BLEEDS! Ya! . . . But before they do, let me ask you a serious question. Are you feeling good tonight? Are you feeling great tonight? Are you ready to party tonight? Are you ready to be FREE tonight? Break all the boundaries tonight? Are you wasted? Are you wrecked? Are you . . . FUCKED UP! Ya! I know I am . . . I know these people down here are feeling pretty good . . . hey don't party too hardy, it's hard to get the puke off the stage!

Remember, T-shirts and refreshments are on sale at the back of the auditorium and remember, please, from me, Ricky Rocket and all the good guys over at XXX. . . . When you leave tonight . . . drive safely!

And now, the band that wants to get inside your head . . . Cerebral Hemorrhage!

Fried-Egg Deal

A man lies on the floor.

(*singing*) ". . . We are the world . . . we are the children!"

(*rolls over and speaks to someone in the first row of the theater*)

Hey there, buddy! How you doin' there, bud? You're my buddy, huh? You got a quarter there for me, bud? You got a quarter for me? Hmmmm?

(*standing*)

I'm sorry. I'm sorry. I didn't mean to bother you, I'm sorry, I didn't see . . . you're all dressed up . . . you're out for a good time . . . you don't want to be bothered by me. . . .

I'll leave you alone. . . . (*turns, then turns back*) You're here with the little lady, she's a beautiful little lady, you're together . . . you're a together guy . . . GOOD FOR YOU! That's what I say. God bless you, that's what I say! Somebody's gotta make it in this world, it might as well be you, right? Good for you, that's what. . . . I'll leave you, I'll leave . . . I'll get outa here. All right. I'll get outa here.

(*turns away, turns back*)

See, buddy, people like me. . . . I'm a loser. . . . Always been a loser, always gonna be a loser. I'm a loser, 'cause I'm a drunk. . . . Always been a drunk. When I was a kid, I was a drunk. . . . When I was a baby, I was a baby drunk.

I'm a good-for-nothin' drunken bum, you shouldn't even look at me. Don't even waste your time. Put me in the trash can and flush it, that's what I say. Just get rid of me. . . . Don't even listen to me, OK, bud? I'm sorry, I didn't mean to . . . I just wanna say: "GOOD FOR YOU!"

You work hard, you deserve everything you got . . . 'cause you beat them at their own game . . . you know? 'Cause you know what? They never give you a straight deal in this world . . . never do. You know what they give you in this world? They give you a fried-egg deal. That's what they give you. A fried-egg deal.

You know what I mean, fried-egg deal? (*flips his hand*) They flip you this way, they flip you that way . . . just like a fried egg, you never know which side you're ending up on. That's the deal, right there. You wake up one morning, you're sunny side up. . . . The next day, you're all scrambled up again, you don't know what's coming next. . . .

And you beat 'em, and I say "GOOD FOR YOU!" Good for you buddy. Me, I'm good for nothin'. I'm good for nothin'. . . . I'll leave you alone. . . .

. . . But you know, I'm good for somethin' buddy. You know why I'm good? I'm . . . good because if . . . if I wasn't where I was . . . you couldn't be where you was . . . 'cause, you know, 'cause (*illustrating with his hands flipping*) you can't have a top without a bottom. It's impossible. It can't be done. You're on the top and I'm on the bottom. We're like two sides of the same coin. See? And you never know which way that coin's gonna flip. . . . (*staring at his flipping hand*) You never know which way that coin's gonna go. . . . That coin there. . . .

(*hand outstretched*) Gotta coin there for me buddy?

(*laughs*)

That's OK, I gotta get goin', I gotta get outa here. It was just a joke, I was just jokin'. . . . I got a limo waiting for me around the corner, don't want him to wait too long. . . . Thanks a lot for listenin' to me, buddy, thanks a lot. God bless you. . . . You're a good guy. . . .

FUNHOUSE

In the winter of 1983 I scraped the bottom. I found myself thinking black thoughts, something like: Shit, it's cold. . . . When am I gonna get a break? . . . One more cup of coffee. . . . Money, need more money. . . . Gotta call that guy about that gig. . . . Hmmm, Phil looked kinda fucked up, hope he's OK. . . . What's a rat doing in my apartment? . . . Yeah, that kiss-ass would get a Guggenheim. . . . And so on. I felt like I was on the outside looking in on my own life. My dream had come true. I was an artist in New York. . . .

And I had to make a new solo for The Public Theater and I couldn't figure out what to make it about. . . .

From the "Alive from Off Center" taping of "FunHouse"

So around eleven o'clock one night, I dropped by Alex's Coffee Shop on the Bowery, picked up two coffee regulars, returned to my studio, turned the lights off (had to, or else the Chinese folks across the street would watch me instead of their TV set) and started pacing back and forth, drinking my coffees. Just like the guys you see on the street. And I tape-recorded what I said and that became the monologue "The Pacer." And that set the cornerstone for *FunHouse*.

Fears. Problems and possible solutions. . . .

FunHouse premiered at the Public Theater in June 1983, directed by Jo Bonney. That fall Fred Zollo and Frank Gero moved it to The Actor's Playhouse, where it ran for two months.

In the Dark

A voice begins in darkness. Slowly lights come up on a man at a table speaking into a microphone.

I wait for dark, the black comes for me. Some people are afraid when the sun goes down. But for me, for me it's good in the deep dark. Warm and dark and close. Some people are afraid of small places, tight spots, restrictive. Not me. I'm in the right place, the good dark place. Like a baby in its womb, like a rat in its hole. . . . I'm OK.

Ever see the black skid marks out on the highway? Ever wonder what happened? I don't. I think about the tires, the rubber . . . the black rubber. Burning. Melting. Pouring down in ropes, in sheets, in long black ribbons all around me. Twisting all around me. Around and around. Black and tight, close and dark. Holding me. Hiding me in the darkness. . . .

Don't you love the smell of black rubber? The way it feels against the skin? Maybe not, it's an acquired taste. Some people never get used to it.

You can work your way up: black leather, then black spandex, then black rubber. Tight. Black. Rubber. Up against you. Pressing. Keeping. Holding. Resilient but firm. Every muscle, every inch is encased in pure black. . . .

The arms, the legs, the chest, the groin, the head. All smooth, all black . . . completely hidden. In my black cocoon I'm where no one can find me, no one can hurt me, no one can touch me. I'm safe in the dark, I'm happy in my hiding place.

I don't have to think, I don't have to feel . . . and the best part is . . . I don't have to see. . . .

Insurance

A man is seated at a desk, talking on the phone.

Hello. Suzy? Hi, Suzy, Uncle Freddy. Is Daddy home? . . . Uncle Freddy. Can you get your daddy, please? . . . Get your father, Susan! Thank you! . . .

Hello, Mr. Stearns, Fred Stanley down at Mutual Insurance! Sorry to bother you around dinnertime, but I was just going over your homeowner's policy and I was kind of shocked to see you don't have very much life insurance. . . . Yes, well, five thousand dollars isn't very much, Mr. Stearns. (*laughs*) I know you don't care what happens after you die, but what about your wife and kids, Mr. Stearns? . . .

Your wife has a job, OK . . . but let's say something should happen and your wife couldn't work? Well, let's say there was a car accident, you were left fatally injured and your wife paralyzed for life? She wouldn't be able to work then, would she, Mr. Stearns? Or, let's say you and the missus go to see a play one night in New York City. You come out of the theater, you get mugged, a gun goes off, you get a bullet in the brain, you're left in a coma for months and months and months . . . wife has to give up her job just to come see you in the hospital. What would happen then, Mr. Stearns? Have you thought about that?

Have you thought about cancer, Mr. Stearns? What about cancer? . . . I know you're having dinner right now, but this might be the most important decision you ever make in your life and I think dinner can wait for five minutes. . . .

. . .

Mr. Stearns, I've seen it time and time again: husband dies, wife's left with no pension, no life insurance, she has a mortgage to pay off. . . . You know, of course, Mr. Stearns, most women in this country outlive their husbands. Hundred thousand widows in this country, Mr. Stearns, hundred thousand! . . . What? . . . No, she probably won't get remarried, Mr. Stearns, very few women do. . . .

Mr. Stearns, follow me for just a second, will you? You die, you're dead, you're in the ground! Mrs. Stearns has no pension, no life insurance, she has a mortgage to pay off . . . little Suzy's in the hospital with some kind of rare bone disease. What happens then? Have you thought about that? Have you thought about it? Do you know how many widows are homeless, Mr. Stearns? Do you know how many homeless women become prostitutes, Mr. Stearns?

I'm not saying that, I'm not saying that, Mr. Stearns. I'm just saying that I know you're a loving father and husband and you only want the best for little Suzy and . . . uh, right! Right! Edwina. Lovely name Edwina . . . and you'd hate to leave Edwina and Suzy unprotected in this terrible and frightening and—let's be honest with each other, Mr. Stearns—perverse and disturbed world we live in today. . . . Why, I could show you street corners in New York where little girls no more than fifteen years old sell themselves . . . and their mothers standing right next to them. . . .

Yes, oh . . . ummm, well, ha ha . . . oh, I'd say around two hundred and fifty thousand dollars' worth would do the trick. . . . Easy terms . . . easy terms, we'll work something out, don't worry. . . . When can you come by? . . . Tomorrow? Tomorrow I'll be here all day. Eleven o'clock? That would be great, Mr. Stearns, I'll see you tomor—what? Oh, don't worry about the cost, we'll talk about that tomorrow. . . . Look, Mr. Stearns, get back to your roast-beef dinner . . . and say hi to, uh, Edwina for me. And Mr. Stearns? . . .

. . . Take care! (*hangs up*)

Inside

A man standing with a microphone speaks in a singsong voice.

OK, gentlemen, this is it, what you've been waiting for, right through that door. Inside, inside! All your dreams come true, don't be blue, this is it, check it out! I said don't wait, don't hesitate. Run don't walk, show's about to start! See it, feel it! Live, living, real. In full color, completely open, fully revealed, "X"-posed for your eyes only! A house of dreams, your very own *Fantasy Island*. If it turns you on, we got it: black, white, red and yellow, boys and girls at your disposal. Men and women behind closed doors! Until you are satisfied! Check it out! Just for you, just the way you want it. You can't do better, nobody offers more. Now, now, now, now, now! No tricks, no substitutions, it's the real thing. A mental orgy, an experience! For you, for them. Lose yourself, immerse yourself in the delirium of total abandon. All the way, all you ever wanted, all you can take! Inside, inside, come right inside and get it. Get it hot! Get it now! Dreams, dreams, dreams, dreams, dreams. . . .

Shit, Fuck, Piss

A bent and craggy man, a Bowery Lear, rails at the storm of filth he lives in.

Fuckin' yer shit, fuck, piss, yer shit, fuck, piss, ya shifugpiss!

What's that!? (*points at floor*) What's that!?!

(*picks up a tiny speck of rubbish on the stage*) It's shit, that's what it is! There's shit on the ground, shit in the air. . . . It's all a bunch of shit if you ask me.

(*to audience*) You know what I'm talking about! You know what I'm talking about! We're living in a cesspool is what I'm talking about. A human trash heap. Everywhere you go there's piles of filth, piles of garbage. You have to step in shit, step in the garbage. In the pools of piss, the streams of piss! The rivers! The rivers are polluted! And the oceans? The oceans are full of dead fish. Dead fish and oil slicks!

And the dead fish wash up on the beaches, see? And then the rats come and they eat the dead fish. And then the cats come and they eat the rats . . . and then the dogs come and they eat the cats . . . and then the dogs, you know what the dogs do? The dogs, they shit all over the place! That's what they do!

. . .

Dog shit and horse shit . . . pigeon shit! (*looks up as he steps backward into an imaginary pile*) Shit, fuck, piss! (*scrapes foot on table edge*) We're living in a toilet, that's what we're doing! Turds in the toilet! I say flush the toilet! FLUSH THE TOILET! FLUSH THE TOILET!

The Specialist

A man stands and talks in a straightforward manner to the audience.

The first piece of equipment you want to make sure you have on hand is a nice big bucket . . . around so big, so deep. (*indicates with hands*) . . . Just fill that up with water. Nice and deep. Right up to the brim. Take your subject by the back of the neck. Firm grip. Bring him over to the bucket . . . and push his head right under the water. Baptize him. Put the fear of God into him. . . . Soak 'im good.

Then up . . . then back down again. . . . Fifteen, twenty seconds is good. Just watch the air bubbles. Air bubbles stop, give it around five more seconds. . . . And back down. Make sure you have a firm grip, sometimes they buck a little. And stay out of the way of the legs, they kick too. . . . Now you have a subject you're ready to work with: he's wet, he's tired and he's scared.

The next piece of equipment you want to have on hand is a nice big metal worktable about so wide, so deep. (*indicates with hands*) . . . I suggest metal just because it lasts longer. Nice big working surface. . . . Get your subject up onto the worktable, strap down the arms, the legs, the head. Piece of gaffer's tape, duct tape, over the mouth and you have him where you want him. Just pinch the nostrils and he can't breathe. He's completely at your disposal. Fingertip control.

OK. So how do we begin? Myself, I like to start with a simple psychological device, kind of a trademark of mine. I'm a smoker, OK? Bad habit, I know I should quit. Anyway, I like to just take the cigarette out, everybody's afraid of fire, take the cigarette out (*indicates with his cigarette*) and just push it right into the navel, soft like wax. . . . Oh, it hurts. It hurts. . . . I'm sure any of you who were in Nam or Korea came across this baby once or twice. Just leave it in there. Kind of an hors d'oeuvre.

What do we want to do for the main course? Well, some people like to work with rubber truncheons, knitting needles, plastic bags over the head, breaking fingers, twisting arms. *Hey!* We're not in the Dark Ages. We have electricity. Electricity when properly applied will achieve whatever ends you desire. Simply take your two electrodes, nothing more than a couple of bare wires hooked up to a generator.

Just take the two wires and press them firmly up against the palms of the hands, the soles of the feet, inside the ear, the eyelids, the nostrils, lips, gums . . . of course, any cavities or fillings you may find. . . . The armpits, the nipples, the genitalia. All very effective. Of course, I know a lot of you have worked with electricity before. So I won't go into a lot of detail.

However, one point I always stress whenever I'm talking about electricity to training groups such as this is that you have a licensed physician on hand, a medical doctor. For two reasons: First of all, he can tell you exactly how much electricity is needed to get the job done. That's his area of expertise, his job. Use him, ask him questions. Secondly, you have a lot of people working around the area, around the electricity. You don't want anyone to get hurt.

. . .

We'll finish up the seminar tomorrow evening. Until then, if you have any questions, please talk to your commanding officer.

(*A phone rings. He answers it.*)

Starving Children

A man strides around the stage with evangelical purpose, addressing the audience with a microphone.

WHAT ARE YOU AFRAID OF? . . . What are you afraid of? . . . The only thing you have to fear is fear itself. . . .

So many people write to me, they write to the station, they stop me in the street, they call me on the telephone. They call me and they say: "Reverend Tim . . . Reverend Tim, I have a problem. My husband's out of work and he's been drinking." "Reverend Tim, I have a problem. My daughter crashed the car up and I think maybe she lost her virginity. . . ." "Reverend Tim, I got no job. . . ." "Reverend Tim, I got no money. . . ." "Reverend Tim, I'm sick. . . ." Problems, problems, problems! And people write to me about them.

I got a letter the other day from a Mrs. R in Seattle that I would like to share with you right now. Mrs. R has a problem that I would like to share with you because I think it tells us so much about how God can help each and every one of us. She wrote me and she said:

"Reverend Tim, I watch your show every day and you are an inspiration to me, Reverend Tim. . . . But Reverend Tim, I have a problem: Ten years ago my boy got back from Vietnam and he was missing a leg. And ever since that time he's been down and lonely and depressed. And now, Reverend Tim, I think he's using heroin, Reverend Tim. And the other day he went out and bought a shotgun, Reverend

Tim, and I'm afraid he might gonna hurt somebody, Reverend Tim, maybe he's gonna kill somebody, Reverend Tim! Maybe he's gonna kill himself, Reverend Tim. Reverend Tim, I'm afraid! Reverend Tim. I'm scared! I'm afraid, I'm scared! . . ."

I read that letter . . . and I got a little angry . . . because I thought to myself . . . Where is the faith? WHERE IS THE FAITH!?! You know we are God's children, we are His sheep. God is our teacher. He's up there to lead us, to help us. God is just settin' up in heaven every day just thinking up new ways to teach us, new ways to test us, new ways to SHOW US HIS LOVE! He just sits up there all day long thinking (He's got nothing better to do). He just says to Himself: "Now what kind of obstacle can I put in their path today that will lead 'em on the right road? What kind of weight can I put on their shoulder that will teach 'em a thing or two?"

(*Tim indicates dropping heavy weights on a tiny individual standing next to him.*) "How's he doing with that? Hmmmm, maybe a little bit more? Just a little bit more. . . ."

AS IT SAYS IN THE BIBLE: "HE WHO CARRIES THE GREATEST BURDEN, HE SHALL KNOW THE GREATEST TRUTH!" Now think about that for a second. . . . It also says: "God helps him who helps himself!"

(*Addressing the camera over the audience*) Mrs. R, sure times are tough, sure life is difficult. Sure you got "problems": your boy's handicapped, he's on drugs, maybe he's gonna kill himself . . . maybe he's gonna kill you . . . but Mrs. R . . . if you've got FAITH. If you've got WILL-

POWER . . . you can make it. . . . I know you can. (*to the audience*) I know we all can.

(*pause*)

Well, so much for our petty personal problems. . . .

I would like to talk to you right now about some little children who carry a burden much greater than any we'll ever know. I'm talking, of course, about the millions upon millions of starving little children in Southeast Asia, in Africa, in South America. Millions upon millions of starving little children.

(*to the camera*) If you're watching at home you can see pictures of them on your TV set. (*to the audience*) Those of you in our audience here can see them up in the monitors. Look at 'em all you want. Aren't they cute? They're starving . . . and they're little.

I want you to think about those starving little children for just a minute. And then I want you to think about that extra piece of pie you had with dinner last night. You weren't even hungry and you had to have that second helping of pie. That extra slice of pie! . . . I want you to think about that MOVIE you went to see, filled with sex and violence. What did it cost you? Five dollars and who knows how much for the hot buttered popcorn! I want you to think about that popcorn. I want you to think about that slice of pie!

. . . And then I want you to think about those little, starving children. And I want you . . . to take out your checkbook. . . . and I want you to write me . . . a check for eighteen dollars. And next month I want you to write me another check. And the month after that and the month after that. . . . Eighteen dollars a month! And you'll be doing everything you can . . . everything you possibly can . . . to help ME do everything I can . . . to help those millions upon millions of starving . . . little . . . children!

Eighteen dollars a month, and you can end starvation in the whole world today. Eighteen dollars a month, and the next time you want an extra slice of pie, just go ahead and eat all you want! The next time you see some poor beggar on the street with his hand up to you begging for a dime, begging for a quarter . . . you can walk on by with a clear conscience 'cause you sent me eighteen bucks! . . . The next time you see some starvin' little baby on the TV set, all withered and bony, with his little stomach stickin' out, you can look all you want and say to yourself: "It's not my fault!"

You know, there are two kinds of people in the world: the haves and the have-nots. . . . And among the haves, there are two kinds of haves: there are those who take out the checkbook, and then there are those who just turn off the TV. . . .

Which one are you?

Sitcom

A man picks up the phone at a table, answering in a shrill, fast-talking voice.

Arnie! Arnie! Yeah, yeah, listen. Sid! You got two minutes? Yeah, yeah, listen, I got a great idea for a sitcom . . . sitcom, Arnie, sitcom! Situation comedy, what are you doing up there in your office, take the straw outa ya nose for two minutes and listen to me for a second. Arnie! Arnie! Concentrate! Follow me.

Scenario: New York City! Apartment building in New York. Black guy lives in the apartment. Nice black guy, middle-class black guy, button-down-sweater type of guy, smokes a pipe. Yeah, yeah . . . harmless black guy. Benson! Benson! We got Benson in this apartment. . . . Across the hall from him, paraplegic kid in a wheelchair. . . . Huh? You don't need a real one, you just get any cute kid and stick him in a wheelchair. What? Fuck the unions! The kid's in a wheelchair here, black guy across the hall. They got a real nice relationship here. Big brother, interracial kind of thing. Yeah. Mushy liberal stuff . . . a show with meaning. . . . Yeah, a show with relevance to the social problems of today. . . . yeah, yeah, *Mary Tyler Moore, Hill Street, M*A*S*H, Cosby, The Waltons!*

Wait, wait, more! Top floor of the building we got a whorehouse! Hookers going up and down the stairs all time of night and day. Falling over the kid with the wheelchair, sticking lollipops in his mouth, patting his head. Cute stuff like that, sweet stuff, light humor, family humor. . . .

Ground flour of the apartment building: gay health club! Homos working out with weights, building up the pectoral muscles. . . . See what I'm saying? We got the beefcake down here doing sit-ups while the cheesecake's up here doing push-ups! Something for everybody! Wait, wait, one more apartment, teen-age kid living with his mother, OK, this is the humor of the show. Kid wants to kill everybody in New York City! One week he makes an atom bomb in his bedroom, next week he puts LSD in the city water supply, then he derails a subway car, who knows? Crazy stuff, funny stuff, hilarious stuff! We'll call the show *Upstairs, Downstairs*. . . . Huh? Who's PBS? Fuck PBS! . . . Those are little people. They don't count. We'll buy the title off of them. . . . Arnie, what are you busting my balls about this thing for? Yeah? That was two years ago! Yeah, I know what's good for me. What's good for me is what's good for you! Arnie, we'll have lunch next week and discuss the project, OK? Huh? Look Arnie, I got a call on the other line, I got to get off. . . . Arnie, I'm getting off. . . . Arnie? . . . Yes, I love you, but I'm getting off. . . . I'm getting off, Arnie! Arnie . . . Arnie . . . Arnie. . . .Good-bye! (*hangs up*)

Calamari

A man sits at a table, speaks in a growly, inner-city voice.

Every time I have fried calamari, I feel like I'm gonna blow up! . . . Vincent, be a good boy and pour your uncle a cup of coffee there. . . . Just a half a cup, no sugar, I'm having a diet. . . .

So Vincent, you go visit Frank in the hospital? How's he doing, he's doing OK, right? Just gallstones, right? I was gonna go visit him last week but I got home from work and I couldn't move! I even bought him a geranium for his room there, but I left it on the Mister Coffee machine in the office and it got all burnt up!

So how's he doing? He's doing all right, huh? Just gallstones, huh? Gallstones is nothing! I saw the whole operation on *Marcus Welby, M.D.* Right on TV they showed it. Very simple operation, I could do it myself. They just make a little cut in the stomach like this . . . then they got this thing, uh like, it's like a grapefruit spoon, OK? They take this grapefruit spoon and they dig out those gallstones. That's all . . . and then they throw 'em away. Throw 'em away right in the garbage. They don't even keep 'em. You figure for the amount of money you pay for that operation they'd at least give you the gallstones to take home . . . show 'em to the kids . . . give 'em to the dog to play with. . . . Forgetaboutit! . . . Merv Griffin had those gallstones one time, he was back on the show in two weeks.

Gallstones is nothing. Of course, when Frank went in, he thought he was gonna DIE! First he thinks he's got appendicitis, then he thinks he's got a heart attack. Then, then they tell him he might be gettin' cancer! And with his mother passing away last year cancer and his brother two years ago cancer! Everybody in that family's dying of cancer! Even the dog died. Remember that little dog they used ta have? The poodle? What was his name there? That cute dog? What was—?

(*interrupting himself, shouting to the back of the stage*)

ANGIE! ANGIE! . . . WHAT WAS THE NAME OF FRANK'S DOG? (*pause*) YEAH, THE ONE THAT DIED! (*longer pause*) . . . Snowball! Snowball! That was it, remember little Snowball? Little pink poodle, they used to dye him all pink, remember that? Lick ya hand? Yeah, he died. . . .

Listen, Vincent, let me have a little piece of that pie there, will you please? Yeah, just a thin piece. Just a thin . . . well, bigger than that for crying out loud, what are you trying to do, starve me to death, come on! . . . And put some whipped cream on top! . . . I don't know what it is, I can't eat a piece of pie without whipped cream on it. . . . It just doesn't taste right. I think you need the cream to lubricate the crumbs, make 'em go down smoother.

Thank you. . . . Huh? . . . What operation? I didn't have no operation. That was an "exploratory," Vincent! An exploratory is not an operation. Exploratory they just open you up, look around inside and close you up again. They don't change nothing. They said I was in perfect health. All I have is a little benign tumor. . . . No, Vincent! Benign! You're thinking of a malignant tumor. Malignant and benign are two different things. Look, malignant tumors are very, very bad for you. But benign tumors . . . benign tumors . . . you can have all the benign tumors you want, they don't hurt ya . . . they're good for ya.

What are you going to do about it anyway? Everybody gets cancer these days, it's in the food you eat, it's in the water you drink . . . that disoksin stuff and the DDT, and the PCB and the acid rain. Every day they think of some new thing put in the food, gives you cancer.

You know, Vincent, it wasn't like this when we was kids! We didn't have all this poison in everything you eat and drink all over the place. . . . Take asbestos. When we was kids we used to have asbestos all over the place. Nobody ever died from asbestos. We used to *play* in asbestos! Nowadays, nowadays you go down to the drugstore to buy yourself some aspirin, some Tylenol, and some maniac put cyanide in the bottle! You take it home and you drop dead! Buy yourself some baby food, it's got ground glass in it! You don't know what you're eatin' anymore. . . .

And if you don't eat nothin', you don't eat nothin', you get that starvation disease . . . uh, you know . . . that starvation disease . . . they uh . . . (*shouts again back over his shoulder*) ANGIE! ANGIE! . . . Well, turn the water off for crying out loud, I gotta ask you an important question! . . . What's she doing in there, washing the dishes twenty-four hours a day! . . . WHAT WAS THE NAME OF THE DISEASE THAT KAREN CARPENTER GIRL DIED FROM? . . . IT WAS IN THE *PEOPLE* MAGAZINE. . . . THE ONE IN THE BATHROOM! . . . YEAH. . . . The anorexia, you get the anorexia! See what I'm saying, Vincent? If you eat you die and if you don't eat you die! I'd rather eat.

Huh? No, I'm not going, I'm not going. Look, I went to the wake, I went to the funeral, enough of these social functions. I mean, Louie was a nice guy and everything, but all we're gonna do is go over to that house and sit around with Mary and talk and eat and besides all Mary's got is a black-and-white TV set! Louie was too cheap when he was alive to buy a color TV and now look what's happened! Mary's stuck with black-and-white for the rest of her life!

Besides, there's a show on TV I want to watch that night. . . . A Charles Bronson movie . . . uh, you know the one . . . the good one, where he's got that big gun and he goes all over New York City and kills all those Puerto Ricans. . . . Yeah, it's a good movie. . . . Nah, I got it on the cable TV, on the cable.

You know what they say, Vince. When you got cable TV you never got to go out. What do I got to go out for? I got everything I need right here: my color TV set, hundred and five stations; my own sofa, nice and soft; my own kitchen, plenty of food in the icebox; my own bathroom, plenty of toilet paper. What do I gotta go out for? Stay home, it's safer, it's cleaner, it's more sanitary. Stay in the house, lock the door, piece of Sara Lee cake, turn on the TV. That's livin'. What else you want from life?

Plus, I just got the videotape machine. Yeah, it's in the bedroom, come on, I'll show it to ya. You can watch whatever you wanna watch whenever you wanna watch it. (*stands*) Like last week Ronald Reagan was on TV, gave that big speech? I recorded the whole thing on my videotape machine! Anytime I wanna watch Ronald Reagan, anytime at all, day or night, middle of the night, BANG! (*hits table*) Ronald Reagan on TV! You can't beat it!

Plus Angie's got that Jane Fonda exercise tape, you know the one? . . . What, me? Forget about it. I'll tell you something though, that Jane Fonda, I wouldn't kick her outa bed! Uh???? (*He starts laughing as he turns to exit. The laughter turns into racking coughs. . . .*)

Make Yourself New!

A bright-eyed, cheery, energetic fellow runs onto the stage.

Hey, how we all doing today? Good? Great!!! Let's all make today a great day! Let's WORK at it! Remember, today's the first day of the rest of your life! If you want something bad enough, you can have it . . . all you have to do is . . . (*throws a wide-arcing fist*) GIVE IT ALL YOU GOT!!!

So are we UP? Are we POSITIVE? Are we ready to CHANGE OUR LIVES? OK! Let's go! (*points to sound booth*) Music, maestro!

(*disco beat starts up, to which he exercises, while shouting to the audience*) Let's start with the bosoms, shall we? Lift and separate. . . . (*limp arm exercises*) . . . And one and two and make yourself new, three and four and do it some more! Only helps if it hurts! And jumping jacks! . . . One and two, if Jane can do it, so can you . . . three and four, burn, baby, burn! Work those thunder thighs . . . you made 'em, you get rid of 'em! . . . And kick, kick, kick, kick. . . . How we doin' with our diets, huh girls? Yogurt (*kick*), grapefruit (*kick*), cottage (*kick*) cheese (*kick*). . . .

Come on, you can do it! CHANGE YOUR LIVES! Come on, it's FUN! (*He kicks a few more times, obviously under a strain.*) Now stretch, stretch, stretch, stretch . . . oh, can you feel that new "you" coming out? (*voice is strained*) I CAN! . . . Sit-ups!!! Time to make your tummy tiny! (*He collapses to the floor.*) One and two and make yourself new. . . .

College of Cashier Education

A smooth-talking, Hispanic disco radio DJ.

Hey, you're listening to Roco, the voice of disco on WFRO in New York City. . . . Let me ask you something: how would you like to earn that big kind of money, huh? Pay all your bills. How would you like to drive a big car, ride in a jet plane? All you gotta do is call the College of Cashier Education! That's right, the College of Cashier Education. Listen to this: You can be a real cashier. Just call CCE and in two weeks you can be cashing in! They teach you everything you need to know, you know? And there's a lot of jobs for cashiers: boutique jobs, supermarket jobs, restaurants, beauty parlors. That's right. Get rid of all your money problems. . . . And if you're a handicapped veteran, don't forget about their special handicapped veteran program. If you served your country and you got trouble getting around, this is the job for you! So get on the phone right now and call the College of Cashier Education at 555-CASH. Tell em Roco sent you. . . . OK, hey, I hope you're all hot and ready for some hot disco dancing 'cause we got the hits for you tonight! I know the girls are hot because I feel hot and when I feel hot everything I . . . (*fade out*)

Honey, I'm Home!

A man is lying on the floor, singing in a raunchy voice.

God bless America! Land that I love! Stand beside her . . . and guide her (*pause*) blah, blah, blah, blah, blah, blah, blah, blah! (*He starts coughing, turns onto his side and notices bystander.*)

Hey! Hey buddy, can you give me a hand here? I just slipped and fell down for a second, could you help me out please? Buddy, pal? How about helping out an old veteran! I served in Korea, buddy! I helped save this country from communism, whaddya say? "Ask not what your country can do for you . . . ask what you can do for your country. . . ."

Remember that one? JFK said that. . . . They blew *his* brains out!

Hey buddy, what do you say? Am I invisible or something? What, am I talking to the fire hydrant here? You! Mister! The guy with the *New York Times* under his arm, how about it? It'll only take you a second. . . . What's a matter, afraid you're gonna miss your bus to Connecticut??? What, do you have to rush home and skim the pool, is that it? Drive the wife to the Amnesty International meeting? Is that why you can't help me up here for a second?

I know you can hear me! I know you can hear me! Don't act like you can't hear me, buddy! I know all about guys like you! Guys like you don't give a fuck about nobody, do ya?

Do ya? You're just a bunch of bums, aren't ya? No good to nobody. . . . You think you're something special 'cause you got a Gold American Express card . . . and 'cause you drink "fine wines." . . . Well, I drink wine too, buddy, nothing special about that! . . .

What are you gonna do? Go home now and have a nice little dinner with the wife and the kids and the dog and gerbil?!? Nice little roast-beef dinner, is that what you're gonna have? Roast beef and gravy??? And little baked potatoes . . . . Maybe some little . . . asparagus tips! Nice little asparagus tips. . . . Is that what you're gonna have tonight? Is that why you can't pick me up? Because you're gonna have asparagus tips tonight?????

(*He begins to get to his feet, very shakily.*) I know all about guys like you! With your London Fog raincoat! And the briefcase that your wife gave you for Christmas with your initials on it and the combination lock! (*pause*) What do you need a combination lock for, you a secret agent or something?

You're all the same, you go home, you walk in the front door and you all say the same damn thing:

(*He's standing now, mimicking the man . . . in a hoarse voice.*) Honey, I'm home! Honey, I'm home! Honey, I'm home!

The Pacer

A man paces and stops, paces and stops, throughout the monologue, talking to himself. He speaks to the audience more directly as the monologue goes on.

Yeah, yeah, yeah, yeah, they're always telling you the same old story, always giving you the same old story: one plus one equals two, two plus two equals four, you reap what you sow. It always starts the same way, it always ends the same way. . . . I don't, I don't, I don't got any answers. . . . I don't know what the answer is. . . .

You're coming and you're going, you're coming and you're going, you take it or you leave it. You make it or you need it. It's human nature, it's human nature, the same old story: man against man, man against nature, man against himself!

Beginning, middle, end. Climax . . . anticlimax. . . . Sub-plot! . . . But you gotta read between the lines . . . you can't win the way things are now. Oh, yeah, sure, sure, sure, sure, sure it used to be all different. Sure when I was a kid, when I was a kid everything was different: Bread, ten cents a loaf. Eggs, fifty cents. No plastic bags. No plastic bags! NO PLASTIC BAGS! Waxed paper! No pollution, no conspiracy.

Everything was different. Easy to understand. I can't understand. . . . I can't, I can't, I can't make any sense out of it. And then the guy, the guy, the guy, the guy says, "Get out of here!" "Get out of here!" . . . "You get out of here," that's what I should of said to him! "You get out of here!" I got no place to go! No place to go! It's crazy, it's a madhouse, a funhouse. . . .

It's dog-eat-dog, man-eat-man, eat or be eaten, hunt or be hunted! It's the letter of the law, the law of the land and the land is jungle! . . . You see what I'm saying, you follow what I'm talking about??? Now, now look, look, look, look. . . . I gotta look after myself first. They want you to give to the taxes, give to the starving children, the abandoned babies, the blind people, the poor people!

I can't worry about those poor people! I gotta worry about me first! . . . And then, then they say, "Don't worry about it! Don't worry about it! We'll take care of you. Everything's gonna be all right! Everything's gonna be terrific! We got a safety net for you! A safety net for you! Jump in the safety net! Go ahead, jump in the safety net. . . . Go ahead, jump. And here's some free cheese to go with you . . . and here's a space shuttle!" . . . I don't want no space shuttle! I just want a cup of coffee!

. . . I give up, I'm gonna give it up! It's just gettin' harder and harder, every day, day in, day out . . . you gotta stand in line, you gotta stand in line for hours and hours and hours. . . . And then you get to the end of the line, you get to the end of the line and they say, "No more!" "No more! We don't got no more for you! . . . No more for you!" For who? For who? Who's gettin' it? Who's gettin' it? I'm not! I'm not gettin' it!

You're either winnin' or you're losin', you're either sinkin' or you're swimmin' . . . and I'm sinkin', see! I'm in a little lifeboat with no oars and I'm sinkin' in the ocean. . . .

• • •

(*indicates with posture*) I'm on a little piece of ice, just gettin' smaller and smaller and smaller day by day by day, goin' into the water . . . and that water's polluted, it's dirty, it's disgusting . . . and I can't swim! I can't swim!

Sink or swim, fish or cut bait! You're either part of the problem or you're part of the solution. . . . And what's the solution? What's the solution? The bomb? The bomb? Drop the bomb. Go ahead, drop it! I don't care! I'm not waiting for any packages! I got no all-paid vacation coming up! I'm no Little Orphan Annie. (*sings in a cracked voice*) "Tomorrow! Tomorrow! Tomorrow!" . . . Where's the tomorrow? You know where tomorrow is? You got a tomorrow? I don't got no tomorrow. . . . OH!!! I know what you're gonna say now. . . . *More! More!* Tomorrow is more . . . that's what tomorrow is. . . . More money. We make more money, everything will be all right, that's it. Let's all make some more money . . . all go to work and make more money . . . and then we can make more kids . . . more people, we need a lot more people! What do we need more people for? What's wrong with me?

More people, more radio stations, we need a lot more radio stations . . . and TV stations, we gotta have more TV stations! Lots more TV stations . . . UHF, VHF, cable TV, satellite TV, mini, maxi, tape deck, PBS, CBS. . . .

(*A loud voice-over of a rock radio DJ comes over the sound system, getting louder and louder.*)

"Hey, this is John Cummings on WXXX, the home of HEAVY METAL! I'm gonna give away ten thousand dollars in the next hour . . . ten thousand dollars in our

MADNESS contest. Bet you could use that money, huh? Well, who knows, maybe you'll win! On the other hand, maybe you won't. (*laughs*) Then you'll just have to SUFFER! And while you're burning in your own private hell, we've got the new AC/DC album for ya right here at WXXX, twenty-four hours a day ROCK-AND-ROLLLLLLL!" (*music begins*)

. . . It never stops, day in, day out. In the subway, the kids with their boxes: *Boom, boom, boom!* In the supermarket, they never shut it off. In the streets. In the elevators. The noise. It never stops. What are they talking about? In my apartment, the people upstairs, always playing that music! (*shouts to the people*) Hey! Turn it down. Hey! I'm trying to think down here! Hey come on!

(*Pacer goes into mad dance which segues into an "air guitar" dance.*)

Shining Star

A man is sitting at a table, leaning forward and speaking into a microphone. His hands are behind his back. Perhaps he is handcuffed. He is lit by a single instrument shining directly into his eyes.

Yeah, yeah, yeah, yeah. . . . I got something to say. I got a few "last words." This is what I got to say: You don't know. You don't know anything about me, you don't know anything about the world, about reality, got it? I mean, who the hell are you people? Who are you to say, "He dies"? What gives you that right? My "peers"? My "jury of peers"? You're not my peers, 'cause I look down on you. You and your fat-ass existence. You and your TV brains. You never been anywhere, you don't know nothin'. . . . All you know is what some idiot on the boob tube tells you.

So maybe I killed those girls . . . so what? I didn't. But what if I did? Insignificant people die all the time. You don't seem to be too concerned when there's a war going on or there's children starving in Africa. What about that, huh? You're responsible for that and you're responsible for putting me away! I mean, first of all, I'm innocent, OK? But second of all, I'm somebody 'cause I have seen the world. I have been in the desert, man, I have seen the "shining star." I have rode with the Kings, man, and I have rode with the best!

I know what the truth is, and the truth is that I count and you don't. It's like when you're a little kid and you step on ants on the sidewalk. You know they don't count. Well, it's the same with me. You're just a bunch of ants. You're not even alive as far as I know. You could just be a bunch of robots. You might be robots filled with blood and guts but you're still robots, see?

See, I can see that. . . . I understand that. 'Cause I have seen the shining star in the desert, man. I have rode a Harley at a hundred and fifty miles per hour and I have seen reality go by! I have been through it. I have tripped in places you don't even know exist! I have shot dope in the Mekong, man. I have looked death right in the eyes, and I saw the Stars and Stripes!

And no one can dispute me! Those who have tried are very sorry now. They're not around to talk about it. 'Cause I'm always ready. . . . There's a war comin' on and this is only the beginning. Only the strong will survive. It's gonna be kill-or-be-killed. Hand to hand. Mind to mind. And I'm ready, see? I'm ready for anything, anything. I passed every test.

See, I will survive 'cause it all passes through me. It's up to me to hold it all together. I am the center. It's like cosmic. Like oriental. You got to go all the way out and come all the way back and keep your center. Like if there was a candle here right now, I could put my hand over it and I wouldn't get burned. I wouldn't. I wouldn't feel any pain at all. 'Cause I can take it, see. I'm just testin' myself harder and harder, goin' out further and further to the shining star. . . .

You people, you people livin' out your safe protected little lives. You think you know about things? You think you can tell me about things? You can't tell me about nothing, man, 'cause I have seen it all. I have shook hands with the devil!

. . .

And you wanna come here and you wanna fight with me and you will lose man, you will lose! 'Cause I am the stronger one, and the stronger one always wins, that's the law of the jungle. That's survival of the fittest. And I am the stronger. I am the stronger physically, mentally and spiritually. . . . (*laughs to himself*)

See, that's the big joke, see? You're just here 'cause I'm here! You just came here tonight to see me! I'm the one! I'm sittin' up here, and you're just sittin' out there scared: "There's the killer. We gotta kill the killer." You're afraid of me, like Jesus! And you think you can just put me away and that's the end of it and that's where you're wrong, man! You can't get rid of me!

'Cause I'm everywhere! I'm in the air, I'm in the ground, I'm inside you. See, 'cause the shining star, it doesn't go away. It's always there in my brain, burnin', shinin' in my head. . . . And when everything's gone, when everything is blowed away . . . I'll still be here!

(*fade to black*)

MEN INSIDE

The best thing about being an actor is that you can be somebody you never were and never would be. Like a soldier. Or a cowboy. Even more interesting is how you figure out how to act like a cowboy. I've never met one in my life. I must have learned how to act like a cowboy from John Wayne, an actor.

Everybody does this, not just actors. Truck drivers act out the stereotypical truck driver. We've all seen them do it. Doctors play-act at being doctors. Yuppies play at being Yuppies. Punks, punks. Lovers, lovers. And so on.

"Men in Dark Times," The Kitchen, March 1982

My problem was that I would go to a movie, come out of the theater and try to make my life work the way the movie worked, with me in the lead role. And then I'd run into a wino acting like Red Skelton, and I'd think this guy was having fun. . . .

So I made *Men Inside* in an attempt to sort out all these people inside me.

Men Inside was first seen at Franklin Furnace in New York in February 1981 and "premiered" at Joseph Papp's Public Theater in July 1982.

Freakshow

Ladies and gentlemen! Step right up and see the freaks. The freak show is about to begin. . . .

Twenty-five cents, two bits, one-fourth of a dollar. . . .

Right behind this curtain, ladies and gentlemen, step right up, come as close as you like, examine them to your heart's content. . . .

See the Fat Lady, the fattest woman in the world! Weigh her on our scales and be amazed! She's huge, a veritable Leviathan!

See the Snake Boy with scalelike skin, there's nothing like him, the eighth wonder of the world!

The Deaf, Dumb and Blind Man, watch him stumble, watch him fall! Fun for the whole family.

The He-She! Is it a man? Is it a woman? Only you can decide!

See the pimply dwarf commit acts unspeakable! Watch him dance with a poodle!

Once in a hundred years, a Negro and a Chinaman mate and we have the Offspring, right behind this curtain, ladies and gentlemen, a medical impossibility.

Yes! Yes! And for the same price, tonight only see Doctor Cyclops, the one-eyed man. He'll give you the cold stare!

. . .

And his friend, the Legless Wonder. He's got wheels instead of legs, wheels instead of legs. A one-man roller derby.

And finally, for the first time in captivity, not an imitation, not a duplication, but the real thing. A genuine, homosexual siamese twin.

Step right up, ladies and gentlemen, step right up. The freak show's about to begin!

Superman!

Little boy leaps off a table, pretending to fly.

SUPERMAN! Duh-duh-duh duh-duh-duh-duh-duh-duh-duh! (*to the Superman theme song*)

Pssssshhhhhhh!!!!!

Hi Dad! I was just practicing my Superman, Dad!

Am I doin' it right, Dad? Am I doin' it right? Hey Dad, guess what I did today? I ran as fast as I could and I threw a rock at a bird and I killed it!

Pretty good, huh Dad?

Hey Dad, when I grow up I'm gonna be just like you, huh Dad? I'm gonna be tall and strong and never make any mistakes and drink beer and shave and drive a car and get a check. I'm gonna be just like you, huh Dad?

Dad, can I ask you a question?

When I grow up I'm not gonna be poor, am I Dad?

Am I?

I'm not gonna be a poor old bum on the street. All smelly and living in a box, am I Dad? I'm gonna be rich like you, huh Dad?

. . .

And . . . Dad? I'm . . . I'm not gonna be a alcoholic, am I Dad? Like Mr. Johnson down the street, never cuts the lawn. I'm not gonna be an alcoholic with a big red nose and throwing up.

And I'm not gonna be a junkie either, am I Dad? Like on *Kojak*. And not have a life worth living and OD all the time. I'm not gonna OD, huh Dad, huh?

Dad? Joey says I'm gonna be a homo! I'm not gonna be a homo, am I Dad? *Homo!* We're not homos, are we Dad?

Dad? NO WAY I CAN BE A NIGGER, HUH DAD, HUH? 'Cause you're not a nigger and Mom's not a nigger, huh? Huh? HUH? We're American, huh Dad?

Dad? I got one more question. When I grow up . . . I'm . . . I'm not . . . gonna . . . gonna go . . . I'm . . . (*begins stuttering and falls to the floor in a fit*)

Nice Shoes

Very friendly, but with growing menace.

Hey . . . hey . . . you . . . you with the glasses. Come here. Come here for a second, I wanna ask you a question. . . . No, come here. I never seen you around the neighborhood before and I just want ta meet ya. . . . What's ya name? . . . Mike? Michael . . . Mike. How ya doin' there, Mike? I'm Sonny, this here's Joey and this is Richie. He's a big guy, huh?

. . . Hey . . . hey . . . hold on for a second, Mike, don't walk away from me when I'm talking to you. . . . Uh . . . I just saw you walkin' around here and uh, I never seen youse before and you're wearing all these nice clothes—Joey! Lookit dis guy's clothes . . . nice clothes. . . . I like the clothes. . . . These are the kind a clothes you wanna be wearin', Joey. . . . Bet you got these clothes up Bloomingdale's didnja?

And the shoes! Nice shoes! I like those shoes, huh? Richie, check out Mike's shoes. . . . I like those shoes, Mike. . . . Hey! You know what we call shoes like dose? "C-Shoes," "C-Shoes." . . . You wanna know why? . . . 'Cause dey cost a C-note . . . hundred bucks, get it?

(*laughing, he turns to Joey*) Pretty funny . . . C-shoes, huh? . . . (*whips around, noticing Mike getting away*)

Hey-hey-hey-hey-hey. . . . Mike, don't walk away from me when I'm talkin' to you here now! That's very impolite, you know? You're being impolite to me . . . and you're embarrassing me in front of my friends. . . . You're insulting me in front of my friends . . . and when somebody insults me I get angry. . . . I get angry and I hurt people . . . heh heh.

RICHIE, SHUT UP! SHUT YA FUCKIN' MOUTH!

Don't listen to him, he's full a shit. I won't let him lay a hand on you. . . . This fight is between you and me. . . .

Look, it's OK . . . it's OK . . . all youse gotta do is apologize to me and everything'll be cool, all right? Just get down on your knees and apologize and—

RICHIE! STAY OUT OF IT! . . . PUT IT BACK. . . . Put the blade back in ya pocket. . . .

Now Mike, look what you started, everybody's gettin' excited around here. Richie's gettin' angry, next thing Joey's gonna get angry. . . . Just get down on ya knees and apologize and then Richie won't think I'm an asshole. . . .

(*condescendingly*) That's great. . . . Just for a second . . . just stay down there for a second. . . . YA NOT A HOMO, ARE YA MIKE? Hey Joey, this guy down on his knees ya think maybe he's a homo? Haha. . . . And do me a favor while you're down there. Just slip your shoes off for a minute, will ya? Joey! Get the shoes! . . . You comfortable there, Mike? You're sure ya not a faggot, are you? You better not be, walking around this neighborhood. We'll castrate ya!

. . .

Here Mike, get up. You don't want to stay down there all day. Let me brush you off. Hey Mike, we're just fucking with ya head. You can take a joke, can't you? Sure you can! I wanna tell you something, Mike: you're good shit. Anytime you need anything in this neighborhood, you just come see me, Sonny, and I'll take care of you, OK? You need fireworks, anything like that, you come see me, OK? OK! (*shaking hands with him*) Well, it was nice talking to you, but we gotta get going, I'll see ya later. . . .

Hmmmm? What? What shoes? (*turning back to Joey*) These shoes? These are *my* shoes, Mike. These are my C-shoes. I just bought these shoes up in Bloomingdale's. Joey? Richie?

(*looks down at Mike's feet*) Oh, you don't got no shoes! Hey Joey, lookit dis guy's got no shoes! Richie, look! . . . Hey, how come you got no shoes? . . . All those nice clothes and no shoes! How'd dat happen? You're gonna get cold with no shoes! Ain't he gonna get cold?

(*laughing right into Mike's face*) Oh! I think we got a crybaby here! I think he's gonna start crying. (*Suddenly Sonny stops laughing, gets a very cold look in his eyes.*) Hey Richie, did you hear that? What was that word he just said?

(*lunging for Mike, grabbing him and talking slowly*) Hey Mike, we don't like swearing around here. Huh? Fuckface? Scumbag? (*fast, dangerous, pulling him up off the ground, so that we can see Sonny's eyes just over his fists*) Hey, hey. You come walking around this neighborhood, embarrassing me around my friends, swearing at me in front of my friends, hey let me tell you something, Mr. Nice Shoes, Mr.

Faggot: You worried about not having no shoes? You're lucky you still got feet! (*pause; he throws Mike to the ground.*) Get the fuck out of here! (*pause*) Asshole! . . . Come on. (*laughing as he walks away with Richie and Joey*) . . . Joey, lemme see my shoes. . . .

Party!

A man bops around the stage, preening.

Yo! I'm standin' on a street corner, I'm lookin' good, I'm feelin' good. I'm thinkin' about sidewalks and saxophones! I'm thinkin' it's a beautiful summer's night. I got on my brand-new clothes. I got me a bottle of wine. I want to go out tonight! I wanna go out and par-tee! I got on my bran'-new shoes (*indicates shoes*), got on my bran'-new pants (*indicates pants*), got on my bran'-new shirt (*models shirt to audience*). Check that shirt out. . . . Qiana, baby. . . . Same as silk, same as silk! Got on my bran'-new "doo," after-shave. (*does a jump and claps his hands*) Um! I'm too good to waste! I wanna go out tonight and party! I want to go dancin'! I wanna go rollerskatin'! I say, Lord above, I am all dressed up tonight, Lord, I am looking good, and I am feeling good. Look at me! Look at me! *You* can't even believe how good I look!

Lord, I need me a little girl. Where's my little girl, Lord? Where's my little girl? Where's my . . . (*He sees the girl of his dreams down the sidewalk.*) . . . There she is jus' a-walkin' down the street! There she is jus' a-struttin' down the street! She got on them high-heeled shoes, swishy skirt, see-through blouse, lipstick, perfume . . . (*inhales the scent of the girl as she passes him along the apron of the stage*) . . . Hey, baby, hold on jus' a minute, where you goin' to? What's your name? You're looking good, and I'm looking good, whatchoo say we go get some Chinese food, go bowling?

. . .

Hey, baby, don't pass me by, I'm the superfly, I'll make you fly. . . . Yo! Sister! I wanna ask you a question: You know what time it is? (*He is now shouting at her retreating figure.*) Yo, sister! Yo, sister! Yo, BITCH, get yo ass back here, I'm talkin' to you! Hey! Come on, baby, whaddya say, we'll have a good time? (*pause*) Yeah, I know your type, twenty bucks, right? (*He turns away.*) Who the hell she think she is? (*turns back shouting*) Who the hell you think you are? Miss America or something? You got no right walkin' around looking like that! Enticing men. . . . Slut! Whore! Prostitute! . . . Ruined my whole evening!

Fantasy

A man sits, bent over, breathing hard.

Slut . . . bitch . . . cunt. . . . Good magazine, yeah. . . . Gina, huh? Virgin, huh? Yeah, I bet you make it with the whole football team. Ya slut. Yeah, spread 'em baby, come on full-color, yeah, let's see 'em. . . . Yeah. . . . Good magazine, yeah. . . .

Yeah. . . . I do it to you, ya slut, I know what you want, huh? I know what kind of guy ya like. . . . I'm gonna make you scream 'cause I'm that kind of guy.

This ya girlfriend, huh? Huh? She's a real blonde, I can see that . . . couple of lesbos, that's what ya are! Whatchoo gonna do with that flashlight, huh? Yeah, I like ya both. . . .

Especially you, Gina, ummmmm, you're nice, Gina. . . . I like you, Gina. . . . I like you, Gina, you're nice. . . . I like you, Gina. . . . I like you, Gina. . . . I like you, Gina. . . . (*coming*) Uhhhhh. . . . I like you, Gina. . . . Uhhhhhh. . . . Ohhhhh! I LOVE YOU, GINA.

Held Down

A man turns quickly, while seated.

Forget it! Just forget it, OK? No, I don't want a neck rub, Cheryl. No, I don't want a back rub either. No, I don't want that rubbed either, I don't want anything rubbed right now, keep your rubbing to yourself. Leave me alone. Don't touch me. . . . I know I know I know. . . . I'm sorry, OK? Is that what you want me to say? I'm sorry. . . .

(*pause*) Listen, Cheryl, we've got to get something straight between us, OK? . . . Every night can't be like last Wednesday night, all right? I have a lot of things on my mind, I've been working hard lately, I'm tired and that party tonight didn't help things. . . . I know, I know, I know it's not important, I know you don't care. . . . I don't care, nobody cares, all right?

It's just sex. What do we need sex for? We're just having a sexual relationship. What do we need sex for? Let's just play Trivial Pursuit for an hour or so. . . . I know I'm being childish. . . . I know. . . . You're right, it happens to every guy once in a while. Every guy once in a while can't. . . . It's normal, it's natural. . . . It happens to every guy. . . . Every guy once in a while, it's normal, it's natural, it happens to every guy. . . . SHIT! It doesn't happen to every guy, it happens to me. It happens to me. It's ME, it's ME, it's ME, it's me . . . and it's you, Cheryl. . . . No, no lemme talk. . . .

At the party tonight you spent the whole night hanging out with Robert in the kitchen. I saw you. Giving him those eyes, those "guess what I'm thinking about" eyes. All right, you're attracted to Robert. I understand. He just got that promotion, he's got a lot of money now, a lot of prestige, power, cocaine. What else could a girl want? Money, power, prestige, cocaine. I know what turns you on, Cheryl, I know because it's what turned you on about me in the first place. And I'm glad Robert got that promotion. Good. It couldn't have happened to . . . I'm glad he got that promotion. Fine. Good. Yes, Robert got that promotion. He got it because he's a back-stabbing, ass-licking slime. . . .

OK? OK? I could have gotten that promotion. I could have gotten it. But see, I have a little problem. I have too much *integrity*, see? I've got too many principles. My problem is that I go into work every day and I sit at my desk and like a sucker I try to do the best job I can. I sit at my desk eight hours a day, knock myself out and everybody sits at their desks and they watch me work. Because they know they're not as good as I am so they're afraid of me, so they watch me. They conspire against me because they're inferior. I am surrounded by a conspiracy of mediocrity just trying to hold me down, hold me down, HOLD ME DOWN, HOLD ME DOWN. . . .

(*Looks at his lap, stops shouting.*)

You know what your problem is, Cheryl? You're insatiable. You're never satisfied. You can't get enough. No guy is good enough for you. He has to be a success in the daytime, he has to be a success at night. He has to be a superman and a superstud. You don't need a man, you need a machine. No wait, I know what you need, you need a real insensitive, male-chauvinist-pig cowboy. That's what you need. With the spurs. . . . Yeah, a real cowboy. . . .

Rodeo

Very fast-paced, jittery, jumping around the stage. High-pitched "cowboy voice."

Whoooooeeee! Boy you shoulda been there, we took that sucker down! It was good, it was real good! (*moves his hands as if he's steering a car*) RRRRRMMMMM!!! Ninety-five miles an hour—BOOM! I hit that Winnebago, guy never knew what hit 'er! Just pushed 'im right off the side of the road.

I'm lookin' in my rearview mirror and I see that guy—he's jumped out of his car, jumpin' up and down, pissed off! I couldn't resist: I bang a U-ey, come back beside him and get out. Guy says to me (*in deep Texas accent*), "Come here boy, I wanna talk to you!" I said, "I wanna talk to you too!" (*a right, a left*) BING! BANG! Guy never knew what hit him! Left enough rubber on that road to make a new set of tires!

I tell you, when it gets goin' that fast and hard I get high! Musta been doin' two, three hundred per. . . . Billy was pullin' 'em so fast he broke a knuckle. . . . You know that Billy when he starts pullin' those beers, pullin' those beers . . . jus' sittin' in the backseat like a hog in a corncrib, suckin' down that brew, half-naked, covered with sweat and stink. . . .

The beer cans rollin' aroun' on the floor and I musta been doing a hundred and fifty m.p.h.! . . . All of a sudden, I see this girl walkin' down the street, right? I couldn't resist. . . .

I hit the brakes and start followin' her in the car, real slow like. Real Playboy-bunny type of girl, you know? I'm followin' real slow, givin' her my "evil eye" and she's jus' a-walkin' down the sidewalk like she don't notice! . . .

All of a sudden, Billy pops out the back window: "Hey baby, hey baby, come 'ere, I wanna kiss your face!" She says, "Kiss my ass!" So Billy, you know what Billy says??? You know what he says? "I can't tell the difference!" I can't tell the difference! Pretty good, huh? That Billy's some kind of comedian, huh? Some kind of comedian. "I can't tell the difference!" WHOOOOEEEE!

(*With no warning, he violently starts miming shooting a rifle three times in three different directions.*) BOOM! BOOM! BOOM! Wished I had a machine gun, coulda killed me even more deer. . . . Killed me three deer, had to leave two behind! Didn't have room on the car for 'em! I jus' took this one big bloody buck, took him and strapped him onto the front of the car, tied him right onto the bumpers. So I'm goin' down the highway, musta been doin' three, four hundred miles per hour. . . . Billy's passed out in the backseat, and the blood starts comin' right up onto the windshield! I had to use my windshield wipers jus' so I could see! (*laughing*)

I come into this gas station—car's all covered with blood, right?—come into this gas station and the boy says to me: "You boys look like you been busy!" Billy hangs his head out the window like some kind of old dog, he says: "Sure have!" and pukes all over the guy's shoes! Whoooooeeeee!!! We know how to have a good time!

Christmas Tree

Middle-aged man, slumped in a chair.

Vinnie, Vinnie, Vinnie, Vinnie. . . . When you gonna get married, huh? When you gonna settle down. . . . You come in here every Monday morning with that bum friend of yours . . . what's-his-name the alcoholic there, what's-his . . . Tommy . . . Tommy the alcoholic! You come in here every Monday morning, you been screwing this chick, you been screwing that chick . . . you been drinking, you been wasting ya paycheck. . . .

Hey, hey, Vinnie, ya twenty-eight years old, you're a bum. . . . You understand me? Uh? You're a bum and that friend a yours Tommy, he's a bum too . . . and my kid Tony, he's a bum too. You're all bums. Bunch a bums. No sense a responsibility, nothin'. My kid Tony, seventeen and a half years old. He's got whatever he wants to have. Upstairs his own bedroom, his own cable TV, Space Invasion . . . seventeen and a half years old he's playing with toys. . . .

For his birthday he wants, he wants a 'lectric guitar, so we buy him a 'lectric guitar. . . . He's down in the basement till two o'clock in the morning playing the goddamn thing. Driving everybody crazy. Dog's barkin', everybody's awake.

You see my LTD out here? Who put the dent in my LTD? Who put the dent in that? Mister Punk Rock. "You got insurance, Dad," he says to me, "you got insurance"! . . . I come home the other day from work, four-thirty in the afternoon . . . he's lying on the couch like some kind of old man. I says to him, "Tony, what are you doin' lying on the couch? Go do your chores!" He says to me, "I did my chores, Dad." I says, "What chores, what chores you do around this house? Tell me, I want to know. . . ."

He says to me, "I fed the dog, Dad." I fed the dog!? I give a shit that dog starves to death! He fed the dog! What is that? He's got no responsibility!

When I was his age, Vinnie, when I was his age every day after school I had to go down to da Big Bear market and load boxes fa a buck an hour, a buck an hour. That was my responsibility. . . . My mother was sick, my brothers was no good. Every day.

And when I got outa high school I got drafted and I went to Korea. You know what Korea was? A war, smart-ass. . . .

I went to Korea and I served my country. That was my responsibility. . . .

And when I come back, everybody I knew was getting married . . . eh! I got married too. . . . I didn't know what the hell I was doin' . . . but I'll tell you something, Vinnie, it was the best thing I ever did in my life. The best thing. And you wanna know why? I'll tell you why. . . .

'Cause a Christmas. 'Cause a Christmas morning. . . .

Christmas morning, ya get up nice and early in the morning, ya know, with ya wife? And ya come downstairs and ya put the presents under the tree, ya know? And ya got the tree all lit up with the little bulbs and the tinsels and the lights dere? I like dose Christmas trees, gifts underneath all nice and shiny. And you have a nice cup a coffee and you have ya bathrobe on, and ya just sittin' dere nice and quiet on da couch with the wife . . . the oil burner's on. . . . And dose kids come runnin' down da stairs all happy and laughin' and da dog's barkin' and everybody's tearin' up dere presents and everybody's happy. And dose kids look up at you and dey love you. Dey love you, Vinnie. . . .

And den and den dere's Christmas dinner and everybody comes over da house. Ya mother and ya brothers and ya sisters and the kids and everybody's sitting around eatin' whatever they want to eat. . . .

And I sit there at that table, Vinnie, and I look at my family and I think to myself: All this belongs to me. This is my house, this is my family, this is my food on the table, goddamned dog on the floor. . . . It's all mine, it all belongs to me, Vinnie. . . .

And it makes me feel good inside, you know. It makes me warm.

That's why you gotta get married, Vinnie, you don't get married you're never gonna have a Christmas tree. Single guys, they don't got Christmas trees. . . .

Looking Out for Number One

A man on a stage talks to a small audience.

I want you all to do something for me right now. . . . I want you to take a look at the person sittin' next to you. Go ahead, don't be shy. . . . And now I want you to answer a question for me: What do you see? Do you see a success story? Do you see a potential millionaire? And what does your neighbor see when he looks at you? What do you see when you look in the mirror in the morning? Do you see a success? S-U-C-C-E-S-S! Success, that is what we are here to talk about tonight. . . .

There is only one person in this world who really matters: yourself! It is your job, it is your daily task to do one very simple and obvious thing: look out for number one. The world follows certain rules, certain laws. . . . And the first law has been the same since Adam and Eve: survival of the fittest! If you want the best for you and yours, you will remember that one fact. . . .

Now, I go to work every day. I'm given a job and I do it, I do it the best I can. . . . I go all over this great country of ours and I talk to people just like you: good, solid, white, middle-class Americans. I talk to them about success. That's my job. At the end of the week, I'm given a paycheck. That money belongs to me. I earned it, I deserve it! I don't ask for charity, I don't ask for a handout! I don't go down to some government office and ask them to pay my bills for me, nosir! I am a member in good standing of the free-enterprise system. (*pause*)

. . .

I used to be ashamed that I owned a big home with a swimming pool. I used to be ashamed that I owned two beautiful cars: a Mercedes, and the Eldorado I saw many of you admiring as you came into the building. . . . I used to be ashamed that my children went to a school free of disagreeable influences . . . that we lived in a neighborhood free of disagreeable influences. . . . I felt *guilty* that we ate roast beef on Sunday afternoons! . . . Well, let me tell you something, friends. . . . We do not live in the Garden of Eden. We live right here on earth! And some will suffer, while others prosper, as it is written in the Bible.

Now, if you could ask the most successful men who ever lived, "What is the secret? What is the secret of success?" Ask Andrew Carnegie . . . ask John D. Rockefeller . . . ask Bob Hope. . . . If you could ask them, what would they tell you? They would tell you that there are two kinds of people in this world: there are the haves and the have-nots. Do you want to be a have? Do you want to look at this world from the bottom lookin' up or from the top lookin' down? 'Cause if you do, if you do you better get out there and you better get a piece of what belongs to you. . . . You want the good things in this world you better get out there, you better hustle! 'Cause if you don't, if you don't, you will be a have-not; and if you are a have-not, you can only lose. . . . If you are hungry, no one will feed you. . . . If you are hurt, no one will take care of you. . . . If a great storm comes from above and destroys the very home you live in . . . no one will replace it, no one will care. Unless you care. Unless you've taken care to take care of number one!

All kinds of people in this world: there are the poor, the foolish, the stupid, the crippled, the elderly. . . . Nothing you can do about them. . . . They've always been around, they're always gonna be around. The bleeding-heart liberals think you should take care of those who can't take care of themselves . . . the haves think you are responsible for the have-nots! You are responsible for only one person: yourself.

You are brought into this world as a single individual, you will live your life as a single individual. You will enjoy your own joy and you will experience your own pain. . . . Life is a struggle, man is an island. . . . Love . . . love, my friends, love is loving yourself first. Thank you, Amen.

VOICES OF AMERICA

By 1982 I was touring more and often found myself in nightclubs. Like when I went on a tour organized by Tim Carr through the Midwest in a big black bus driven by a black guy named Blackbird. Also on tour were the Rock Steady Crew, one of the first break-dance groups, and Fab Five Freddy, a rapper/artist. In this pre-*Flashdance* era, Crazy Legs and Frosty Freeze would start jumping around and all the jaws would go slack.

"Bernie" from "Drinking in America," 1986

I had made *Voices of America* as a kind of vocal exercise, and found it was good to do in places where people didn't speak English or were drunk. Like clubs. The idea was to do it very fast and loud.

Pretty much standard "comedy" fare, I include it here for copyright purposes. Too many people have stolen the stuff already.

Voices of America premiered at Van Lagestein's Corps de Garde in Groningen, Holland, in April 1982.

WXXX

Fast, smooth, modulated.

Hey, we've got fifteen lucky winners every hour on the hour here at WXXX ROCK RADIO! (*singers: "W-X-X-X!"; sound effect*) Karen Sousa just won twenty-five dollars and free tickets to see the STONES at the Meadowlands this weekend. Say "Hi!" to Mick for me, Karen! Remember, there's winners every hour on the hour AND we'll be giving away the MADNESS (*horn*) TEN-THOUSAND-DOLLAR PRIZE sometime this week. Listen in, answer the question of the day and YOU may be a winner! I'm John Cummmmmmmmmings and we'll be rockin' out all afternoon! (*singers: "W-X-X-X! MORE MUSIC!"*) We've got the request line open and . . . WHAT!? Oh, I'm supposed to ask the question NOW? OK, here's the question. . . . If you had a choice of dying from a NUCLEAR HOLOCAUST (oh, no!) or a HEROIN OVERDOSE (oh, wow!), which would you choose? Just joking! The question is: Dum-de-de-dumm-dumm-da! WHAT is KEITH RICHARD'S hairdresser's name? Know the answer? OK, OK . . . donnnnn't tell anybody! We're keeping the lines open and the first fifteen listeners to call in will WIN tickets to see the STONES and a chance at the MADNESS (*horn*) TEN-THOUSAND-DOLLAR PRIZE. . . . Buys a lot of balloons. (*buzzer*) Gotcha! Hey! It's two-thirty, school's out, it's a beautiful day, well I promised it to you, I said I'd have it and listen we're gonna HAVE that EXCLUSIVE . . . John . . . Lennon . . . interview. . . . Just minutes before he died. It's coming up in the next hour. . . . But first . . . a word from Ernie. . . .

New Action Army

A young male voice.

Hey! Can I ask you a question? Are you a confused young guy? Don't know where you're going? Can't find a job? Lonely?

How'd you like a job where you travel all over the world, learn a skill, wear a uniform, meet a bunch of great guys and even earn a little money?

If your answer is "Yes!" you might be the kind of guy we're looking for for the NEW ACTION ARMY. . . .

How'd you like to handle a real weapon? See the world? PLUS you get a uniform that's recognized just about everywhere . . . and you meet a bunch of great guys who like to have fun and drink.

The best part is, it's exciting . . . you're risking your life twenty-four hours a day.

So whaddya say? The army's a lotta fun! Come on and be a part of it!

The New Action Army—Where the Action Is!

(*deep male voice tag*)

Call your local recruiter for details today.

Sale, Sale, Sale!

Very, very fast, loud, nonstop.

Sale, sale, sale, sale, sale, sale! Come on down girls, we've got great savings, great buys 'cause it's SUMMERTIME DOLLAR-DAYS DISCOUNTS this month at ZEEBO'S Department Stores!

Ready for summer barbecues? We are, with nifty hibachis, fully automatic gas-driven barbies, electric charcoal cookers and portable turning spits. All on sale with colorful matching accessories: racks, forks, aprons, lawn chairs. Start your garden now. We've got seeds, hoses, shovels . . . all you add is the elbow grease. . . . But make sure you're dressed right: we've got sunhats, sea socks and sand shoes on sale now! Watch the figure, girls: sexy squeeze girdles, and extra-sharp pointed Dar-dee uplift padded underwire support bras, disposable nylon stockings, on sale now! And for Junior, matching play clothes, pail-and-shovel set, harness and tether! Don't forget Dad: We've got tools for the car, adjustable liquor cabinets and, just in this week, bowling shoes and fabulous fishing hats! Granma wants to come along? She'll need a cane, maybe a wheelchair . . . all on sale! We've got realistic leatherette bones for Fido, electric guitars for the young rockers, and fully automatic submachine guns for Uncle!

Sale, sale, sale, sale, sale, sale! We've got barbecues galore and all the trimmings 'cause it's Summertime Dollar-Days Discounts this month at all Zeebo's Department Stores!

Better hurry!

Li'l Doggie Dog Food

Deep Texas drawl, Rawhide.

(*sound effect of cattle*)

HEYAAAH! HEYAAAH! Git on there, li'l dogies!

(*dog bark*) Hi there, fella! (*bark*)

(*chuckle*) Being a working cowboy is no easy job. . . . I'm roping cattle from sunup to sundown, keeping those lil' dogies in line. . . . That's why I got my partner here, King. (*bark*) . . . Heh heh. . . . He works hard too!

At the end of the day, when I'm ready to eat a nice big steak, well you know, King is pretty hungry too. . . . (*bark*) Heh heh. . . . That's why I give him Li'l Doggie Dog Food—all meat, chunks of beef! Hell, he's around those cows all day long . . . you bet he wants to eat one! (*bark*)

That's why he gets the real thing, the best thing: pure, one hundred percent, grade-A, all-American prime beef! Those Hindus won't touch it, but hell, my dog sure will!

(*bark*) My dog's a working man . . . he deserves to eat like a man. Doesn't your dog deserve the same? Li'l Doggie all-beef dog food—for the little man in the house. . . . (*bark*) Heh heh . . . HEYAAAH!!! (*cattle sound*)

Real Italian

This is Mario at Mario's Real Italian Restaurant.

We got clams! We got lobsters! We got spaghetti, anchovies, lasagna, soup de jour! We got the best cooks in town, the best sauce, the best garlic bread.

And don't forget Mario's "Mama Mia" salad bar with all the radishes, carrots, shrimps, Bac-o-Bits, lettuce, cottage cheese, swiss squares, celery sticks, swedish meatballs, cucumbers, croutons, and ten different dressings you can eat!

You wanna eat? You wanna eat till you die? Come on down to Mario's Real Italian—Route 115 and the Old Colony Turnpike behind Bamberger's in Paramus!

We'll feed you like your mama used to! *Mangia!*

(*new voice*) Open for lunch and dinner. All major credit cards accepted!

WFRO

Smooth Latin accent.

Let me ask you something: Are you in a dead-end job? Don't you wish you were a rich guy? Don't you wish you had the good things in life? A nice car. A big stereo. A hot chick? Hey, if you were a radio announcer you'd have them. Because radio announcers have a great time—look at me: Roco; I'm the proof, baby!

OK, you want to become a hot DJ—you better get on the phone and call the NBC school for radio broadcasting. They have a special three-week course, tells you everything you need to know, you know? And then, they help you get a job! Hey, and if you're a veteran, you may be eligible for their special handicapped veteran program. So stop wasting your time, call the NBC Radio Announcers School right now at 212-555-7757. . . . Hey, and tell 'em Roco told you about it, OK?

OK! You're listening to Roco, the voice of disco on WFRO. I hope you are all out there hot and ready for some hot disco dancing because we got the hits for you tonight! . . . I know the girls are HOT, because I feel HOT and when I feel HOT everything I touch gets HOT and I'm touching some hot new record, just came in today, you be hearing it this weekend at the DISCO. . . . This is the Hell's Kitchen Gang . . . bringing it home to you, mama. It's called "Watch the Red!"

Watch the Red!

Done as a rap, with a beat.

I said "Watch the Red! Watch the Red! Watch the Red! Watch the Red!"

Best keep watchin' till you lose bread,

Said I rock you here, I rock you dere,

I rock you right outa your underwear!

I said some are hot, and some are cold, but

I keep a-rockin' till I'm rock-and-rolled

Said Uptown, Downtown, 'Roundtown Saturday Night,

If you don't know which way is up, baby you ain't too bright!

This is a story without much glory, it happened just the other night,

I was in the big city, feelin' real pretty, stopped at a traffic light. . . .

A chick walked by, I said my, my . . . that lady is outasight

The girl's chunky but funky, she's movin' I'm groovin'

I wanna go PARTY tonight!

So I says to the dame, What's your name, Lady Jane?

I'm the superfly, I can make you fly

How 'bout a movie, or somethin' groovy?

Chinese food? Or a Quaalude. . . . Are you in the mood? Are you in the mood?

I gunned my engine, I wanted attention and I wanted it right away!

But she kept walkin', she heard me talkin', but man, that chick was gay!

Life in the city, it sure ain't pretty
It gets me down, this crazy town
It's makes me feel so blue, like I'm in a zoo
Like I'm in a cage, like I'm in a rage
I wanna pull the plug, take a slug
End it all, 'cause I feel real small
I feel all alone, I got no home,
I might as well be livin' in the twilight zone!

Fat Fighter

Fat-fat-fat-fat-fat-fat-fat. . . .

Take a look in the mirror, what do you see? A slim, shapely, sensuous woman? A woman who attracts men when she walks down the street?

Or do you see fat?

Around the neck, around the thighs, around the waist. . . . What about your wrists, your ankles, your cheeks? Look carefully, fat is everywhere. . . .

If you're fat, you need help. You need . . . FAT FIGHTER, the new proven formula that dissolves fat as it accumulates. Now you can eat as much as you like all day long and not gain a pound. Just take two FAT FIGHTERS before you start eating, then eat ice cream, cake, candy, butter, potato chips, spaghetti, beer, thick cream soups, pies, heavy breads, french fries, syrups, puddings, lard, milkshakes, fudge, chocolates, pancakes, waffles, pâté, oil, grease, pizza, cookies . . . and not gain a pound!

Fat Fighter is all you need . . . and it's guaranteed. . . .

And remember, FAT FIGHTER contains no harmful ingredients, just pure one-hundred-percent dextroamphetamine sulfate.

FAT FIGHTER . . . when you're FAT FAT FAT!

The Crash

(*Station ID voice: "More music-XXX!"*) Yeah . . . hey, we still got a couple a minutes on the MADNESS phone and while we're waiting for your call . . . hey, you know one of my favorite political rock groups today is The Crash. Yeah . . . really make me think about things, you know what I mean? I listen to their lyrics and I get mad . . . they're real. And we've got a real surprise for you, a real recording of The Crash when they were playing that great benefit concert for all the starving people in . . . uh . . . wow, I forgot where! Anyway, it was great, they're great, and this is one of their great songs: "We're Not Gonna Take It Anymore. . . ."

(*Live concert-audience effect: cheering, whistles, etc. Man with Cockney accent addresses the audience.*)

Thank you. Thank you. (*spits*) Thank you. This next tune is dedicated to all the people fighting in El Salvador, Northern Ireland and the South Bronx. It's called "We're Not Gonna Take It Anymore!"

(*screaming*)

I said a one, two, three, four—we're not gonna take it anymore!

Five, six, seven, eight—(*knocks*) We're knocking, knocking at your door. . . .

(*chorus*) Who's there? Who's there? Who's there?
Better let us in, or we'll blow it in!

With guns in hand we'll roam the land. . . .
We'll find the cheats with their Parliament seats. . . .
We'll knock 'em down and we'll hang 'em high. . . .
And they'll say "My, my!" as they slowly die. . . .
I said a one, two, three, four!

Thank you . . . thank you . . . thank you. . . .

Twenty-five Top Dead

Twenty-five top dead recording artists—rock, pop, jazz, folk, new wave: all DEAD, all GOLD, all IMMORTAL!

(*music collage over*)

BUDDY HOLLY!

This is a limited-time offer, a special two-album set of the greatest hits by the greatest martyrs of music. All dead, all gold, all immortal.

Just listen to what you get! John Lennon!

But that's not all! You also get Janis Joplin, Jimi Hendrix, jazz great John Coltrane. Yes, you get Phil Ochs, Mama Cass, Elvis Presley . . . and who can forget Mario Lanza. . . .

Also Sid Vicious, Darby Crash, Tim Buckley, Duane Allman and Berry Oakley. Grateful Dead's Pigpen, Otis Redding, James Honeyman-Scott, Mark Bolan and the entire T-Rex. . . . Yes you get Bob Marley, Harry Chapin, Eric Dolphy. . . . Twenty-five top dead recording artists, all GOLD, all DEAD! Yes, you get Jim Morrison, AC/DC's immortal Bon Scot, Keith Moon, Brian Jones, Richard Farina, Nat King Cole and who can forget Eddie Cochrane?

Led Zeppelin's legendary Jon Bonham. . . .

This special memorial album is not available in record stores, only through this special TV offer for only $19.95!

Call toll-free, 1-800-555-7757, or send check or money order to:

MUSIC MARTYRS! PO Box 25, John F. Kennedy Station, NY, NY 10099.

Act now and receive your special bonus comedy album: John Belushi and Lenny Bruce "Live!" This is a limited-time offer, it may not be around tomorrow, call today!

UNCOLLECTED

Occasionally I will work on a monologue for some time, only to find that it doesn't fit the needs of the longer solo performance. It becomes an orphan.

I have collected some of these monologues here. They are raw. They have not had the benefit of repeat performances.

The narrator from "The New World," Dance Theater Workshop, 1981

"Confession," "Dope" and "Just Business" were destined to be part of *Drinking in America* and never made it. "A Great Bunch of Guys" was originally performed as a voice-over to a slide show in *Men in Dark Times* (1982). "The Stud" was part of the touring solo entitled *That Girl* (1980). "The Throat" and "Alone Together" showed up in *Advocate*, an X-rated collection of pieces at Artist's Space (1983). And "The Quiet Man" was removed from *Fun House* in its first run at The Public Theater.

Confession

In the name of the Father, the Son and the Holy Ghost, Amen. Dear Lord . . . forgive me for I have sinned. I have done many bad things this past week. Things that I am almost afraid to confess. . . . O Lord Jesus, have mercy on my poor soul. Please show me the love that you have shown for the vilest leper and the most wretched whore. . . .

Jesus, I have sinned. I have been drunk twice this week. And while I was drunk, I smoked a lot of cigarettes and I swore. I told a story that mocked black people and that made fun of a woman's breasts. . . .

Jesus, I have sinned. After I was drunk, I drove home and I broke the speed limit and tried to run over a dog. And I took your name in vain. Jesus, forgive me.

And Jesus, I have been gluttonous too. On Thursday night while I was watching TV I ate an entire carton of ice cream, two bags of potato chips and eleven Slim Jims.

Also I have been lecherous, Lord. The same night I watched the Mandrell sisters on television and imagined them naked and making lesbian love to one another. . . .

And Jesus, a man in my office was promoted over me, and I wished that I had the promotion instead. And I cursed him.

But Lord, my worst sin is hard for me to say. . . . I had a fantasy, Lord. I had a fantasy about that guy in the office. I had a fantasy that he and I were alone together after work. And when he turned his back to me, I grabbed a pencil from my desk and stabbed him in the neck. And when he fainted, Lord, I tied his feet and hands to the desk. Then I poured lighter fluid over him, Lord . . . and . . . and while he was burning I popped his eyes out with a letter opener. Then I broke the blade off the paper cutter and sawed off his arms and his legs while he screamed. Then I ground the pieces up in a paper shredder and flushed them down the toilet. Then I took his still screaming torso and compacted it in a trash compactor. . . .

O Lord, forgive me, I have sinned. . . .

Dope

Mellow, hip voice.

Okay man, come on up. . . . Don't worry. Don't worry! The dog's in the bedroom. . . . I promise she won't bite you, I just fed her. Just come on up. . . . You don't have anyone with you? Good.

So what do you need? I got Thai stick, Hawaiian, Jamaican and Napa Valley. . . . The Hawaiian is very green, gives a very clean, fast head. And it's strong. The Jamaican is more mellow, more colors. I wouldn't buy this domestic unless you're having a big party or something and you just need a lot of industrial-grade smoke around. . . . The Thai is good. Thai is always good. Guy who gets it for me actually goes to Bangkok to pick it up. . . . Really. . . . He's very cool, been doing it for years. . . . Keeps all his money in precious jewels. Says he'll take me someday. . . . I know what you like. . . . If I were you I'd go with the Hawaiian. You can't go wrong with Hawaiian. You won't fall asleep, but it's very strong. One hit. Yeah. Here, I'll roll one, you can try it. . . . And you want a quarter, right? Cool.

What else can I do you for? Heh heh. . . .

No problem. Yeah, a gram doesn't last too long these days. . . . I've got two things, actually the same thing, but not really: I've got pink Peruvian flake, excellent. Here take a look, excellent, you can see the color . . . lovely stuff. . . . That's powder, probably has some cut in it, I never cut it, but that's the way it comes and you never know. . . .That's a C-note a gram for that. Simple, straightforward blow. . . .

Then I've got the rocks. These are real rocks, very clean, very pure. . . . A guy I know shoots and he only does this stuff . . . no adulterants whatsoever. Two hundred a gram. . . . Well, this is close to pure, that's why. This is the blow that a certain first-baseman used to do . . . follow my drift? Smoking coke . . . yeah. Go for it. You only live once. Here, let me weigh it up. You'll see it comes to a lot.

What else do you need? 'Ludes? I got pharmaceutical 'ludes. . . . Ecstasy? . . . Have you tried it yet? I'm waiting until this weekend, go to Palladium and flip out. Should be nice. . . . Valiums I got. Tuinals, got trouble sleeping? . . .

Hey, wait a minute, I got something you have to try . . . this is very special . . . have you ever tried heroin? . . . No, I know, I feel the same way, but this is different stuff, this is pure.

The heroin you read about is that street shit. . . . Half the time it isn't even heroin, it's quinine mixed with barbiturates or powdered methadone or one of those things.

I'm talking about USDA-approved, grade-A, puro heroin. This stuff just doesn't exist anymore. And I know what you're thinking, because I was thinking the same thing: No needles for me, thank you. But see, that's what junkies use 'cause they do that garbage street stuff. This is pure, this is like what a doctor would give you in the hospital. It's completely different. Much more like opium, and you know opium's cool. And you don't shoot it, see? No, you don't

snort it either. . . . You smoke it on a piece of tinfoil. Very clean and sanitary. It's good for you, lets you get into your head. . . .

Here, just try a little bit, it won't kill you. It's very nice, it's like smoking very mellow weed. Check it out. . . .

Just Business

Man on the phone. Hearty, big voice.

Yeah, OK, put him on . . . yeah. . . . JACK! How ya doin'? Yeah . . . yeah. . . . Doin' real great. . . . Yeah, she's good, so's the kids . . . yeah. . . .

What's on your mind . . . what can I do for you? . . . Yeah. . . . Yeah, I know. . . . Yeah, it's kind of sticky. . . . Yeah (*stretching as he talks*) . . . Yeah, I can see what you're saying. . . . Well, but, yeah, Jack. . . . Jack, I think it's great that you're sticking up for the guy, I mean I really appreciate it, I really . . .

It's good to hear your point of view, Jack, you know I respect your opinion on things. . . . Yeah. . . . Yeah . . . but listen, Jack. . . . Jack, I like Barry too, OK, but I had to let him go because, look, he's just not . . . yeah, but he's not producing, Jack! He's not profitable. . . .

Jack, the guy's fifty-nine years old and he doesn't come in and do a day's work! We all gotta pull our weight around here. . . . Jack, the amount of money I'm paying him, I can hire three kids out of college who will hustle and break their little behinds right in two! Start 'em at 22K and watch 'em run!

Bushy tails and bright eyes are what I need, Jack, not the Geritol and shuffleboard set. What do I need the guy for? Yeah, I like the guy too. I've known him for twenty-three years. Our kids played ball together. . . .

. . .

Yeah, but he, uh, Jack, LISTEN. . . . NO, he doesn't give me any alternative! I didn't want to fire him. I offered him a job in shipping, but he turned me down! He said he couldn't take the pay cut! Well, now he's got a pretty big pay cut if you ask me!

I know, I know . . . it's tough, but what else can I do? I can't pay a guy sixty-five thou a year to sharpen pencils and goose his secretary! I know he's got a pension coming up. . . . Well, Jack. . . . WHAT DO YOU WANT ME TO DO, FOR CRYING OUT LOUD? I'M NOT IN THE FUCKING WELFARE BUSINESS! I'M IN A PROFIT BUSINESS HERE!

Yeah, yeah. . . . Look, can I talk for two seconds, OK, please? Can I get a word in edgewise? All right, well just, follow me for a second, OK, just follow this logic, will ya? . . .

You like, you like that place you just bought up in the mountains? You like your swimming pool? You like that Mercedes station wagon your wife drives? You like having your kid in Exeter? Jack, listen, that stuff costs money and there's only one thing that makes money for you and that's this business.

Now, if you want to tell me that you want to trade your job for his job . . . because . . . BECAUSE THAT'S EXACTLY . . . THAT'S EXACTLY WHAT . . . THAT'S EXACTLY WHAT YOU'RE DOIN', JACK!

Jack, if we're not making money in this place I can't pay anybody, can I? Now, if you want to take a pay cut so I can keep Barry, be my guest . . . but that's the way the cookie crumbles and I'm sorry. I really am. You gotta look out for number one or there ain't gonna be no numbers at all, kid. . . .

Look, I got a call coming in in a few minutes so I better get off the phone. . . . I appreciate you sticking up for Barry, Jack, but in a funny way that makes me want to get rid of him even more, because now he's wasting *your* time as well! And I can't have people wasting time in this company . . . yeah . . . yeah. Well, lemme tell you, Jack, anytime you want a job in the personnel department. I can arrange it. . . . Just joking! Just joking! Yeah. Yeah. I know it gets a little out of hand sometimes, it gets a little crazy, I know. We've all been working hard. Yeah.

Yeah . . . I know. I know. . . . No, I don't blame you. OK. Yeah. So . . . so . . . say "Hi" to Jeanette for me, all right? Yeah. OK. OK. Yeah. Yeah. . . . OK . . . OK. . . . Yeah. . . . Bye. . . . Bye, Jack. OK . . . Yeah, you too!

(*hangs up*)

A Great Bunch of Guys (from MEN IN DARK TIMES)

Every day, me and da fellas used ta get tagetha and go down to da docks. Dey were a bunch a hot shits, you know whud I mean?

Dere was Angie and Tony and Vinnie and Vito and me. Every day we'd go down ta see if dey had any woik for us. Some days dey did, and some days dey didn't. When dey did, we'd woik all day hauling coffee beans or tuna-fish heads or some shit like dat. For a buck an hour . . . a buck an hour.

But dat wasn't such bad money den. Nobody had any money and dey was honest. Not like dese crooks and bums you see around da streets dese days. Dey don't know da meaning a woik.

Some days we couldn't get no woik, so we'd hang around. Maybe, if Tony had some money—'cause he was kinda rich since his fadda had a grocery store—if Tony had some money, we'd go and buy donuts at da donut factory. We'd always make Vito ask for 'em, 'cause Vito stuttered and he had ta practice talkin', ya know. Except we all thought it was pretty funny.

Anyway, Vito died in da war. We all went over, but Vito was on da front and he got a bullet true da neck. Den we all came back afta da war and we didn't have nuddin' ta do. It was like a depression except nobody cared and we was all gettin' money for sittin' on our asses anyway.

. . .

Den Tony got married, den Angie got married. So I said, "Shit, what da hell!" and I got married too. Vinnie went ta college, da smart-ass. Den he got into da movies. Sometimes I see him on da late show. He always plays goombas, usually a criminal or sometin'.

So now, Angie's got cancer and once in a while I see Tony afta church when I get a paper at his store.

I don't know. It's funny. Dey were a bunch a great guys.

The Stud (from THAT GIRL)

A man addresses the audience in a slow, confident drawl.

Sometimes, when I'm in a bar, having a drink with some guys, one will make an idle comment like "How does he do it? He always has the girls. . . ."

I remain quiet when I hear such remarks. I tend to keep a low profile with regard to my "extracurricular activities." I don't need to advertise, I know what I've got . . . and the girls, they can tell by my eyes . . . they know what I've got. . . .

I'm not so good-looking. I was athletic when I was younger, but no Mr. Universe. I'm medium height and medium weight. I've never really excelled at anything, certainly not school, and as far as my job goes, they can all fuck themselves.

But you know what? I don't care. 'Cause I've got what every guy . . . and every woman wants . . . and all the looks, brains and money in the world can't buy it—I'm "endowed." I've got a long, thick, well-shaped prick. The kind girls die for. . . .

You're laughing. So what? Fuck you. Facts are facts. I'll hang out in a bar down on Wall Street around six or seven o'clock and in come the girls. The ones I like are the business types, the ones with their suits and big bow ties and Adidas. Shit. I'll wear a jacket and tie, nothin' fancy, I want 'em to know my politics. One way or the other I say a word or two to the chick and we end up either having another drink or splitting.

. . .

They love to tell me about their boyfriends and lovers. About what wonderful men they are. So nice, so gentle, so dependable . . . so boring. And they love to tell me what a wonderful cock I've got, so big, so hard, so unlike anything they've got at home. And to top it off, I've got a special surprise: I don't come for a long, long time . . . and when I do, there's more to follow. . . .

Ever see a girl cry 'cause she's so happy? Ever see a girl beg to take another look? Ever see someone faint because she's had such an intense orgasm? . . .

I have. . . .

Let's face it, sex is what everyone is basically interested in. Everybody wants great sex with great-looking great fucks. And there are only so many. And I am one.

It's like in college when I studied what's-his-name, the Greek guy, Plato. He said that everything in the world has a perfect example after which it is modeled. Platonic perfection, that's my sex life.

Don't tell me about love, I got love. I always keep the best for daily use, that's love. . . . I got love . . . and I got all the others too. . . . I see a girl walking down the street who appeals to me, next thing I know, I'm doing her . . . and she's loving it.

Some of 'em get scared after a while and go back to their boyfriends, that's fine with me. Some get addicted, I get rid of them too. One girl told me she was gonna kill herself. . . . Never did find out what happened. . . .

. . .

But most of the time they are very cool about it. Whenever I call 'em up, they drop whatever they're doing, whatever they're doing, and come to me. A couple of times girls have stopped fucking their boyfriends when I called. See, they understand that this kind of quality and quantity is in limited supply. . . .

I don't give out my phone number, I don't need the aggravation. No I don't need the aggravation . . . just the good part. . . .

The Throat (from ADVOCATE)

Spoken formally.

I am constantly amazed, almost frightened, by the sensitive complexity of the human physical plant. The human body, that is.

Consider the throat. Normally used for transmitting air, food and speech, it is the body's most vital highway. It is nothing less than the path between heart and mind. And it must be kept in perfect working order, clean of debris, lubricated, warm and nourished.

It is esthetically pleasing as well. For the neck is one of the most graceful and erotic parts of the body. The slightest touch on the throat brings feelings of titillation and pleasure.

The throat is such a sensitive thing. A small disorder can cause a sore throat—or worse, a diseased throat. Fever and pain set in and, if they persist, the throat becomes a source of intense irritation.

It becomes the sole center of conscious attention. Imagine for a moment a canker in the throat. Sore and open. Deep inside. Burning. Or many cankers, inflamed and bleeding. The throat becomes dry as the pain increases. It is impossible to swallow.

Then the discovery that the cankers are malignant. Cancer of the throat. Life-threatening, it must be removed. Perhaps the vocal cords are destroyed in the process; a hole is left. A new voice is created. The whole personality changes. Crippled . . . perhaps no voice at all. Mute.

The throat is very vulnerable. It must be protected at all costs. Imagine being punched in the throat. Or strangulation. Asphyxiation. Tighter and tighter, then blackout.

A piece of wire is all that's needed. But perhaps the worst of all is the most spectacular: the slitting of the throat with a straight razor.

One deft move, deep and quick. The wound is fatal, yet consciousness persists. . . .

Alone Together (from ADVOCATE)

A man stands deep in the corner of the stage, almost mumbling, in a kind of "aw shucks" manner.

Hello, remember me? I'm right here where you left me. Right in that dark corner. . . . I've been waiting. . . .

Come on, gimme a smile. You owe me that. After all this time. All my memories. . . .

Wait, nothin' to be scared of. You know me . . . harmless. Nothin' but a joke. Always was, always will be. . . .

You didn't think I was gonna stay way back there forever, did you? Huh. Pushing my broom. Hauling the big roller trash cart filled with used-up pint-sized milk cartons, scribbled paper, broken pencils, apple cores. . . . No, not forever. . . . Huh. . . .

You may have forgotten me, but I remember. When you've got the time, you remember everything. . . .

I even kept your picture. See? . . . Oh, you don't want to look? You don't like it? I do. I look at it all the time. Nice outfit . . . nice colors, school colors, right? I know. . . .

It catches you just the way. That way you used to be. That smile. That laugh. I remember your laugh very well. Seems like you were always laughing. . . . You used to laugh at me kinda, huh?

. . .

Wait a minute, you just got here. . . . I wanna ask you. . . . You still that way? You're not laughin' now. You seem pretty serious now. . . . Why are you so serious?

We can have some fun. . . . It's just you and me down here, you know. . . . Funny you should come down here after all these years. But you know, I've always been here. Always. . . .

Wait . . . I know . . . we can tell each other stories. . . .

Well . . . about things that have happened. I bet a lot of interesting things have happened to you since then. You were always so interesting. You always had such interesting things to say. . . . What? Sure, I heard you talking. . . . And I remember every word. You and your friends had so much to say in those days, so young . . . so satirical. . . . Huh?

I have a good memory. For stories.

Like one time, I was down here. All alone. Just about where you're standing right now, near that damp spot, and I heard this noise. . . . Just a little noise. In the wall there. . . . Scratchin'. Something scratchin' against metal. . . . I almost stopped breathing.

Then I pulled that piece of metal back. . . . Very slowly. As careful as I could. I looked in and it was dark, of course.

Up jumps this rat, right at my face. . . . That was all it was. A rat. I killed it in one kick. Just a rat . . . huh.

. . .

It was so quiet down here and that rat went and bothered me with its scratchin'. Disturbed me, you know.

Like just now, it was real quiet and peaceful . . . and then, what do you know, there you were.

Just like it was yesterday. . . .

The Quiet Man (deleted from FUNHOUSE)

A man speaks to the audience in a very sincere, direct and quiet manner.

This is my place. Welcome to my place. This is the place where people come to watch people. People love to watch people, don't you think? I know I do. . . . There are so many, the variety is endless.

I can't imagine anything finer than a sunny Sunday afternoon in the park where I can just sit and watch the world go by. The young couples in love. The sturdy joggers. The pretty girls. And the children. I especially love to watch children playing. . . . The way they sort of tumble along, singing and laughing in little voices. . . . Everything is exciting and amusing, everything is new to them. Everyone's their friend.

"Little people." It's a miracle that hands could be so small and perfectly formed. Eyes so bright. Skin so fair. They haven't a care to wrinkle their small brows.

(*pause*)

Sometimes, one will come close by where I sit. Perhaps a little girl of nine years or so will come and quietly look at me. I can almost picture her now, the little rosebud of a mouth, the tummy thrust forward, the knobby knees peeking out from under a frilly dress. An angel come to visit.

. . .

How I memorize each feature as she stands before me; each gesture, each breath. If I sit very still, she might even speak to me. This is when I must be very gentle, careful not to scare her.

"Would you like to sit down?" I might ask.

She turns to see if Mother's watching, and then, like the little lady she is, she places her sweet bottom on the bench beside me. Then she asks me: "How old are you?" and I just smile. . . .

She reaches out and touches my hand, curious, yet so cautious. If I am really lucky, she doesn't let go.

We hold hands and watch the world go by together. . . . I look down at her shining hair, her barrette . . . the tiny, immaculate ear, the slender neck. So fragile. . . .

What could be better than this? To be so close to pure hope. . . .

(*pause*)

The mother calls. And my little friend, forewarned about the peril in our illicit love, runs off. . . .

As I wave good-bye.

A Note on Performance

Each piece takes place in a very spare set. Two chairs and a microphone and microphone stand for *Drinking in America*; a table, chair and table mic for *FunHouse*; one chair for *Men Inside*; a mic on a micstand for *Voices of America*.

1979

I always wear the same thing: black pants, a white oxford button-down shirt (sometimes a white T-shirt) and black ref shoes.

The idea is to perform athletically. Jump around. Scream and shout. Knock myself out. Go from one piece to the next rapidly and without pause.

I have a wide vocal range, which I make broader using a microphone. I usually "fake" some kind of accent: Texan, Southern, Black urban, Italo-ethnic . . . what feels right.

Many of the monologues address the audience directly, usually behind some conceit, like lecturing or preaching. Occasionally I'm speaking to another person, but the amount of pantomime used to indicate that person is kept to a minimum.

I try to keep what I'm doing and what the character is doing in the same plane. I never make believe I'm doing anything, like driving a car. I'm not a mime. It's too distracting for the audience.

I try to get as close to the reality of the character as possible using only my voice, posture and inner feelings. Sometimes I feel the guy is standing next to me.

About the Author

Eric Bogosian was raised in Woburn, Massachusetts, and received a degree in theater from Oberlin College. In 1976, shortly after he came to New York, he began performing his solo pieces, and in 1982 and 1983, *Men Inside* and *FunHouse* were produced at the Public Theater. *Drinking in America* opened on January 20, 1986, at the American Place Theatre and won Bogosian a Drama Desk Award for Outstanding Solo Performance, and an Obie Award for Best New Play. An abridged version of the piece was shown on Cinemax. His new solo, *Sex, Drugs and Rock 'n' Roll*, will be shown on HBO in the coming year.

Bogosian has appeared in films and on television, and is currently writing a dramatic work for the Public Theater and a screenplay.